Appliance Cooking

D1051581

Jean Paré

www.**companys**coming.com
visit our web-site

Front Cover
1. Very Berry Juice, page 80 **(Juicer)**
2. French Bread Pizza, page 148 **(Toaster Oven)**
3. Monte Cristo Sandwich, page 118 **(Sandwich Maker)**
4. Berry Rhubarb Dumpling Dessert, page 138 **(Slow Cooker)**
5. Tropical Breeze, page 82 **(Juicer)**
6. Ribs Delight, page 102 **(Pressure Cooker)**

Back Cover

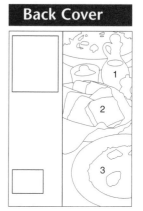

Back Cover
1. French-Type Dressing, page 22 **(Blender)**
2. Boston Brown Bread, page 122 **(Slow Cooker)**
3. Curried Beef And Barley, page 33 **(Electric Frying Pan)**

Appliance Cooking

Copyright © Company's Coming Publishing Limited

Second Printing April 2001

Canadian Cataloguing in Publication Data

Main entry under title:
    Appliance Cooking

Includes index.
ISBN 1-895455-90-1

    1. Cookery. 2. Kitchen utensils. 3. Kitchen appliances.

TX652.A66 2001   641.5'8   C00-901545-0

Published also in French under title: Recettes pour appareils de cuisine
ISBN 1-895455-47-2

Published simultaneously in Canada and the United States of America by
COMPANY'S COMING PUBLISHING LIMITED
2311 - 96 Street
Edmonton, Alberta, Canada T6N 1G3
Tel: (780) 450-6223   Fax: (780) 450-1857
www.companyscoming.com

Cooking Tonight?
Drop by companyscoming.com

companyscoming.com

| Who We Are | Browse Cookbooks | Cooking Tonight? | Home |

everyday ingredients

feature recipes

feature recipes —— Cooking tonight? Check out this month's *feature recipes—* absolutely FREE!

tips and tricks —— Looking for some great kitchen helpers? *tips and tricks* is here to save the day!

table talk —— In search of answers to cooking or household questions? Do you have answers you'd like to share? Join the fun with *table talk*, our on-line question and answer bulletin board. Our *table talk chat room* connects you with cooks from around the world. Great for swapping recipes too!

cooking links —— Other interesting and informative web-sites are just a click away with *cooking links.*

experts on-line —— Consult *experts on-line* for Jean Paré's time-saving tips and advice.

keyword search —— Find cookbooks by title, description or food category using *keyword search*.

e-mail us —— We want to hear from you—*e-mail us* lets you offer suggestions for upcoming titles, or share your favorite recipes.

Company's Coming
COOKBOOKS

everyday
recipes trusted
by millions

Company's Coming Cookbooks

Original Series

- 150 Delicious Squares
- Appetizers
- Appliance Cooking
- Barbecues
- Breads
- Breakfasts & Brunches
- Cakes
- Casseroles
- Chicken, Etc.
- Cookies
- Cooking for Two

- Desserts
- Kids Cooking
- Light Casseroles
- Light Recipes
- Low-Fat Cooking
- Low-Fat Pasta
- Main Courses
- Make-Ahead Meals
- Meatless Cooking
- Muffins & More
- One-Dish Meals

- Pasta
- Pies
- Pizza!
- Preserves
- Salads
- Slow Cooker Recipe
- Soups & Sandwiche
- Starters
- Stir-Fry
- The Potato Book
- Vegetables

Greatest Hits Series

- Biscuits, Muffins & Loaves
- Dips, Spreads & Dressings
- Italian **NEW** *May 1/01*
- Mexican **NEW** *May 1/01*
- Sandwiches & Wraps
- Soups & Salads

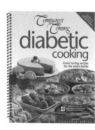

Lifestyle Series

- Diabetic Cooking
- Grilling
- Low-Fat Cooking
- Low-Fat Pasta

Special Occasion Series

- Chocolate Everything

Table of Contents

Blender

Bread Machine

Hand Blender

Juicer

Slow Cooker

Index

Tips Index

Survey

Company's Coming Story 6

Foreword. 7

Blender 8

Bread Machine 24

Electric Frying Pan 33

Food Processor 48

Hand Blender 67

Juicer. 79

Pressure Cooker. 92

Sandwich Maker 114

Slow Cooker 122

Toaster Oven. 139

Measurement Tables 151

Index. 152

Photo Index. 156

Tip Index. 157

Mail Order Form 159

Survey. 160

The Company's Coming Story

Jean Paré grew up understanding that the combination of family, friends and home cooking is the essence of a good life. From her mother she learned to appreciate good cooking, while her father praised even her earliest attempts. When she left home she took with her many acquired family recipes, a love of cooking and an intriguing desire to read recipe books like novels!

"never share a recipe you wouldn't use yourself"

In 1963, when her four children had all reached school age, Jean volunteered to cater the 50th anniversary of the Vermilion School of Agriculture, now Lakeland College. Working out of her home, Jean prepared a dinner for over 1000 people which launched a flourishing catering operation that continued for over eighteen years. During that time she was provided with countless opportunities to test new ideas with immediate feedback—resulting in empty plates and contented customers! Whether preparing cocktail sandwiches for a house party or serving a hot meal for 1500 people, Jean Paré earned a reputation for good food, courteous service and reasonable prices.

"Why don't you write a cookbook?" Time and again, as requests for her recipes mounted, Jean was asked that question. Jean's response was to team up with her son, Grant Lovig, in the fall of 1980 to form Company's Coming Publishing Limited. April 14, 1981, marked the debut of "150 DELICIOUS SQUARES", the first Company's Coming cookbook in what soon would become Canada's most popular cookbook series.

Jean Paré's operation has grown steadily from the early days of working out of a spare bedroom in her home. Full-time staff includes marketing personnel located in major cities across Canada. Home Office is based in Edmonton, Alberta in a modern building constructed specially for the company.

Today the company distributes throughout Canada and the United States in addition to numerous overseas markets, all under the guidance of Jean's daughter, Gail Lovig. Best-sellers many times over, Company's Coming cookbooks are published in English and French, plus a Spanish-language edition is available in Mexico. Familiar and trusted in home kitchens the world over, Company's Coming cookbooks are offered in a variety of formats, including the original softcover series.

Jean Paré's approach to cooking has always called for quick and easy recipes using everyday ingredients. Even when traveling, she is constantly on the lookout for new ideas to share with her readers. At home, she can usually be found researching and writing recipes, or working in the company's test kitchen. Jean continues to gain new supporters by adhering to what she calls "the golden rule of cooking": never share a recipe you wouldn't use yourself. It's an approach that works—*millions of times over!*

Foreword

Do you want dinner ready when you get home from work? Are quick hot lunches and speedy snacks a way of life for your busy family? *Appliance Cooking* is jam-packed with delicious recipes that are quick and easy to prepare for everything from the faithful slow cooker and pressure cooker to the more modern juicer and hand blender.

Recipes and cooking tips are provided for 10 common counter-top appliances. Each appliance has its own section, beginning with a general description of the appliance used to test the recipes that follow. Although the recipes will most likely be successful with other models, we encourage you to read your own instruction manual beforehand and compare.

If you want steaming hot grilled sandwiches oozing with stuffing, pull out your sandwich maker for spur-of-the-moment lunches or casual suppers. When you want a hearty stew or roast pronto after work, your pressure cooker will serve up tender, juicy meat in a fraction of the cooking time. For make-ahead convenience, throw ingredients into your slow cooker before you leave in the morning and walk in the door hours later to tantalizing aromas.

Get all your vitamins and nutrients in a flavor explosion with freshly squeezed fruit or vegetable juice made with your juicer. (Keep your friends guessing at the ingredients!) The blender or hand blender are great for making a variety of cocktails, shakes and slushes as well as dressings and sauces, but reach for your food processor for more involved preparation such as pizza dough or pesto.

Whether savory or sweet is your choice, bread machines are an easy way to enjoy the aroma and taste of fresh, home-made loaves. Serve the bread with a one-dish meal simmered in your electric frying pan. And when summer hits, or small quantities are all that you need, the economical toaster oven heats up quickly and keeps your kitchen cool.

Enjoy effortless creations with more than 170 kitchen-tested recipes in *Appliance Cooking*!

Jean Paré

Each recipe has been analyzed using the most up-to-date version of the Canadian Nutrient File from Health Canada, which is based upon the United States Department of Agriculture (USDA) Nutrient Data Base.

Margaret Ng, B.Sc. (Hon), M.A.
Registered Dietician

Blender

Blenders are a cinch for chopping, puréeing and liquefying food. The following blender recipes were tested with a 5-cup (1.25 L) capacity model, featuring 3 pulse speeds (grate, chop and grind), plus 5 continuous-speed settings (stir, purée, mix, blend and liquefy). Read your owner's manual to learn about your model's features and limitations. For example, some models can crush ice but others cannot. For best results, cut fruits, vegetables or meats into ½ to 1 inch (1.2-2.5 cm) size pieces first. Stop blending often to check the size of pieces or to scrape sides of pitcher, ensuring proper mixing.

Crêpes

Because there is no sugar in these, they are suitable for either sweet or savory fillings. Can also be made in a food processor, using knife blade.

Large eggs	3	3
Cooking oil	1 tbsp.	15 mL
All-purpose flour	¾ cup	175 mL
Salt	¼ tsp.	1 mL
Milk	1 cup	250 mL

Put all 5 ingredients into blender in order listed. Cover. Process until smooth. Batter consistency should be like thick cream. A bit more milk or flour can be added to obtain proper consistency. Grease 6 or 7 inch (15 or 18 cm) frying pan (bottom measurement) and heat on medium. Add 2 tbsp. (30 mL) batter, quickly tilting pan to coat bottom. Batter won't spread if pan is too hot. When edges start to brown and top loses its shine, remove from pan to plate or waxed paper to cool. Store in plastic bags in refrigerator for up to 3 days. To freeze, place waxed paper between each crêpe. Thaw in wrapping to prevent drying out. Makes 2 cups (500 mL) batter, enough for 16 crêpes.

1 crêpe: 51 Calories; 2 g Total Fat; 62 mg Sodium; 2 g Protein; 6 g Carbohydrate; trace Dietary Fiber

Pictured on page 17.

Blender Hollandaise

Everybody's favorite!

Egg yolks (large)	4	4
Lemon juice	2 tbsp.	30 mL
Cayenne pepper, just a pinch		
Salt, just a pinch		
Butter (not margarine)	1 cup	250 mL

Put first 4 ingredients into blender. Cover. Process for 5 to 7 seconds.

Heat butter in small saucepan until bubbling. With blender running, slowly pour butter through hole in lid, blending until thick and fluffy. Use immediately or hold in top of double boiler over hot water. Makes 1⅓ cups (325 mL).

2 tbsp. (30 mL): 177 Calories; 19.4 g Total Fat; 181 mg Sodium; 1 g Protein; trace Carbohydrate; trace Dietary Fiber

Béarnaise Sauce

Just enough bite and thickness.

Egg yolks (large)	3	3
White vinegar	1 tbsp.	15 mL
Lemon juice	1½ tsp.	7 mL
Green onion, chopped	1	1
Dried tarragon	1 tsp.	5 mL
Parsley flakes	½ tsp.	2 mL
Salt, sprinkle		
Pepper, sprinkle		
Butter (not margarine)	½ cup	125 mL

Put first 8 ingredients into blender. Cover. Process for about 10 seconds.

Heat butter in small saucepan until bubbling. With blender running, slowly pour butter through hole in lid. Blend until thickened. Makes ¾ cup (175 mL).

2 tbsp. (30 mL): 167 Calories; 18 g Total Fat; 162 mg Sodium; 2 g Protein; 1 g Carbohydrate; trace Dietary Fiber

Sundried Tomato Pesto

Delicious on grilled chicken breasts and over hot pasta.

Dried tomatoes (not packed in oil), cut in quarters, packed	1 cup	250 mL
Boiling water	⅔ cup	150 mL
Vegetable bouillon powder	1 tsp.	5 mL
Whole garlic clove, peeled	1	1
Olive oil	½ cup	125 mL
Fresh basil leaves, packed	1 cup	250 mL
Fresh oregano leaves, packed	2 tbsp.	30 mL

Put tomatoes, water and bouillon powder into blender. Let stand for 5 minutes. Cover. Pulse with on/off motion until tomatoes are chopped.

Add garlic clove and olive oil. Process until tomatoes are quite small.

Add basil and oregano leaves. Pulse with on/off motion, scraping down sides as necessary, until thick and quite smooth. Makes 1¼ cups (300 mL). Freeze 1 tbsp. (15 mL) in ice cube trays. Store in freezer bags. Makes 20 ice cubes.

1 cube: 58 Calories; 5.9 g Total Fat; 33 mg Sodium; 1 g Protein; 2 g Carbohydrate; 1 g Dietary Fiber

Pictured on page 18.

SUNDRIED TOMATO PESTO SPREAD: Stir a thawed cube into an 8 oz. (250 g) package of cream cheese.

Pictured on page 18.

 Process large recipes in small batches in your blender to control texture and protect the motor.

Berry Cooler

Pretty mauve shade, and just sweet enough.

Frozen blueberries	½ cup	125 mL
Non-fat blueberry (or fieldberry) yogurt,	⅔ cup	150 mL
Milk	¾ cup	175 mL
Vanilla	⅛ tsp.	0.5 mL

Put blueberries into blender. Add yogurt, milk and vanilla. Process until smooth. Serve immediately. Makes 2 cups (500 mL).

1 cup (250 mL): 117 Calories; 1.5 g Total Fat; 110 mg Sodium; 7 g Protein; 19 g Carbohydrate; 1 g Dietary Fiber

Pictured on page 17.

Variation: Use strawberries or raspberries in place of blueberries. Use strawberry or raspberry yogurt in place of blueberry yogurt.

Vegetable Topper

Besides being a great topping for baked potato or cooked vegetable, it can be used as a dip.

Creamed cottage cheese	1 cup	250 mL
Non-fat plain yogurt	¼ cup	60 mL
White vinegar	1 tbsp.	15 mL
Dill weed	½ tsp.	2 mL
Onion powder	¼ tsp.	1 mL
Granulated sugar	1 tsp.	5 mL
Salt	½ tsp.	2 mL
Pepper	⅛ tsp.	0.5 mL

Put all 8 ingredients into blender. Process until smooth. Makes 1¼ cups (300 mL).

2 tbsp. (30 mL): 24 Calories; 0.3 g Total Fat; 239 mg Sodium; 4 g Protein; 2 g Carbohydrate; trace Dietary Fiber

Blender

Orange Freeze

Extraordinary, flavorful, fresh tasting and cold!

Milk	1⅓ cups	325 mL
Granulated sugar	⅓ cup	75 mL
Frozen concentrated orange juice	½ cup	125 mL
Vanilla ice cream	1 cup	250 mL
Ice cubes	6	6

Put first 4 ingredients into blender. Cover. Process until smooth.

With blender running, add ice cubes, 1 at a time, through hole in lid until mixture is smooth. Serve immediately. Makes 3½ cups (875 mL).

1 cup (250 mL): 265 Calories; 5.4 g Total Fat; 83 mg Sodium; 6 g Protein; 50 g Carbohydrate; trace Dietary Fiber

Lemon Slush

Quickest of the best.

Fresh lemon juice (about 3 medium lemons)	½ cup	125 mL
Granulated sugar (or more to taste)	½ cup	125 mL
Water	½ cup	125 mL
Crushed ice (or 12 ice cubes)	2 cups	500 mL

Put all 4 ingredients into blender. Process until slushy. (If using ice cubes, add, 1 or 2 at a time, through hole in lid. Process until slushy.) Serve immediately. Makes 3 cups (750 mL).

1 cup (250 mL): 145 Calories; 0 g Total Fat; 1 mg Sodium; trace Protein; 39 g Carbohydrate; trace Dietary Fiber

Blender

Grape Chill

Tastes like a grape-flavored creamsicle. Yummy!

Frozen concentrated grape juice	2 tbsp.	30 mL
Milk	¾ cup	175 mL
Vanilla ice cream	2 cups	500 mL

Put all 3 ingredients into blender. Process until smooth. Serve immediately. Makes 2 cups (500 mL).

1 cup (250 mL): 358 Calories; 16.2 g Total Fat; 172 mg Sodium; 8 g Protein; 46 g Carbohydrate; trace Dietary Fiber

Frosty Peach

This blends up fast and easy.

Non-fat peach yogurt	1 cup	250 mL
Frozen concentrated orange juice	1 tbsp.	15 mL
Canned peach halves (or fresh)	2	2
Ice cubes	6	6

Put yogurt, concentrated orange juice and peach halves into blender. Process until smooth. With blender running, add ice cubes, 1 at a time, through hole in lid until slushy. Serve immediately. Makes 2½ cups (625 mL).

1 cup (250 mL): 90 Calories; 0.3 g Total Fat; 75 mg Sodium; 5 g Protein; 18 g Carbohydrate; 1 g Dietary Fiber

PEACH BANANA FROST: With blender running, add 1 small banana, sliced, and 2 to 3 more ice cubes through hole in lid until slushy.

Paré Pointer

A Scotland yard is 36 inches, the same as here.

Banana Orange Milk Shake

A favorite shake. So refreshing.

Frozen concentrated orange juice	½ cup	125 mL
Vanilla ice cream	1 cup	250 mL
Medium banana, sliced	½	½

Put all 3 ingredients into blender. Process until smooth. Serve immediately. Makes 1⅔ (400 mL) cups.

1 cup (250 mL): 345 Calories; 9.4 g Total Fat; 77 mg Sodium; 6 g Protein; 62 g Carbohydrate; 1 g Dietary Fiber

CHOCO BANANA SHAKE: Omit orange juice. Use chocolate ice cream. Add ½ cup (125 mL) milk and 1 tbsp. (15 mL) chocolate syrup.

PEANUT BANANA SHAKE: Omit orange juice. Add ½ cup (125 mL) milk and 1 tbsp. (15 mL) peanut butter.

Pineapple Shake

Be sure to try the variations so you can pick a favorite.

Can of crushed pineapple, with juice	14 oz.	398 mL
Milk	1 cup	250 mL
Lemon juice	2 tsp.	10 mL
Vanilla ice cream	2 cups	500 mL

Put pineapple with juice into blender. Add milk, lemon juice and ice cream. Process until smooth. Makes 4½ cups (1.1 L).

1 cup (250 mL): 207 Calories; 7.4 g Total Fat; 84 mg Sodium; 5 g Protein; 33 g Carbohydrate; 1 g Dietary Fiber

PINEAPPLE PEACH SHAKE: Add 4 peach halves (fresh or canned, drained).

PIÑA COLADA SHAKE: Decrease milk to ½ cup (125 mL) and add ½ cup (125 mL) coconut milk.

Strawberry Milk Shake

Looks attractive. Nice flavor.

Milk	1 cup	250 mL
Frozen whole strawberries, halved before measuring	1 cup	250 mL
Vanilla ice cream	1 cup	250 mL
Lemon juice	½ tsp.	2 mL

Pour milk into blender. Add strawberries, ice cream and lemon juice. Process until smooth. Serve immediately. Makes 2½ cups (625 mL).

1 cup (250 mL): 176 Calories; 7.4 g Total Fat; 101 mg Sodium; 6 g Protein; 23 g Carbohydrate; 1 g Dietary Fiber

Egg Nog

The egg in this nog is cooked! Add more cinnamon and nutmeg to taste.

Milk (see Note)	1 cup	250 mL
Liquid honey	1 tbsp.	15 mL
Vanilla	¼ tsp.	1 mL
Hard-boiled egg	1	1
Ground nutmeg, just a pinch		
Ground cinnamon, just a pinch		
Ice cubes, chopped	2	2

Put all 7 ingredients into blender. Cover. Process until smooth. Makes 1¾ cups (425 mL) with foam.

½ cup (125 mL): 72 Calories; 2.3 g Total Fat; 55 mg Sodium; 4 g Protein; 9 g Carbohydrate; trace Dietary Fiber

Note: For a creamier egg nog, use whole milk.

Banana Daiquiri

As refreshing as being in the Caribbean. Thick, smooth and slushy!

Ripe medium bananas, cut into 1 inch (2.5 cm) pieces	2	2
Lime juice	2 tbsp.	30 mL
White or light rum	¾ cup	175 mL
Icing (confectioner's) sugar	2 tbsp.	30 mL
Ice cubes	16	16

Put first 4 ingredients into blender. Cover. Process for 10 to 20 seconds. With blender running, add ice cubes, 2 or 3 at a time, through hole in lid, scraping down sides as necessary, until ice cubes are blended smooth. Add as many ice cubes as necessary to make thick and slushy. Makes about 2½ cups (625 mL).

⅔ cup (150 mL): 171 Calories; 0.3 g Total Fat; 1 mg Sodium; 1 g Protein; 18 g Carbohydrate; 1 g Dietary Fiber

VIRGIN BANANA DAIQUIRI: Omit rum. Add 2 tsp. (10 mL) rum flavoring and ¾ cup (175 mL) water or milk before processing.

1. Margarita Slush, page 20 **(Blender)**
2. Frozen Strawberry Daiquiri, page 19 **(Blender)**
3. Crêpes, page 8 **(Blender)**
4. Very Berry Syrup, page 88 **(Juicer)**
5. Berry Cooler, page 11 **(Blender)**

Props Courtesy Of: Le Gnome
Proctor-Silex

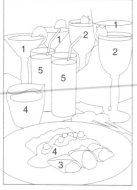

Frozen Strawberry Daiquiri

Very, very strawberry.

Sliced frozen strawberries	1½ cups	375 mL
Water	2 tbsp.	30 mL
White rum	3 tbsp.	50 mL
Lime juice	1 tsp.	5 mL
Icing (confectioner's) sugar	2 tbsp.	30 mL
Ice cubes	6-8	6-8
Whole fresh strawberries, for garnish	2	2

Put first 5 ingredients into blender. Cover. Process for 30 to 40 seconds until smooth.

With blender running, add ice cubes, 1 at a time, through hole in lid, scraping down sides as necessary, until ice cubes are blended smooth.

Spoon into champagne glasses. Garnish each glass with whole strawberry. Serve immediately. Makes about 1¾ cups (425 mL).

⅞ cup (200 mL): 117 Calories; 0.1 g Total Fat; 3 mg Sodium; trace Protein; 18 g Carbohydrate; 2 g Dietary Fiber

Pictured on page 17.

VIRGIN STRAWBERRY DAIQUIRI: Omit rum. Add 1 tsp. (5 mL) rum flavoring and 3 tbsp. (50 mL) water before blending.

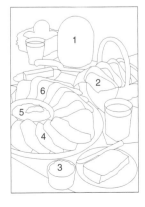

1. Maple Wheat Bread, page 25 **(Bread Machine)**
2. Orange Poppy Seed Bread, page 29 **(Bread Machine)**
3. Sundried Tomato Pesto, page 10 **(Blender)**
4. Herb Bread, page 32 **(Bread Machine)**
5. Sundried Tomato Pesto Spread, page 10 **(Blender)**
6. Pumpernickel Bread, page 25 **(Bread Machine)**

Props Courtesy Of: Winners Stores

Margarita Slush

Cool, tangy and delicious.

Salt (optional)		
Fresh lime, cut into small wedges	1	1
Can of frozen concentrated limeade	12½ oz.	355 mL
Tequila	¾ cup	175 mL
Triple Sec liqueur	¾ cup	175 mL
Ice cubes, approximately	20	20
Lime slices, for garnish		

Dampen rims of glasses. Dip rims in salt. Garnish glasses with wedges of lime.

Put limeade, Tequila and Triple Sec into blender. Cover. Process for 5 seconds. With blender running, add ice cubes, 2 or 3 at a time, through hole in lid, scraping down sides as necessary, until ice cubes are blended smooth. Add as many ice cubes necessary to make thick and slushy.

Spoon or pour into salt-rimmed glasses. Garnish each glass with lime slice. Makes about 5 cups (1.25 L).

¾ cup (175 mL): 303 Calories; 0.2 g Total Fat; 2 mg Sodium; trace Protein; 46 g Carbohydrate; 0 g Dietary Fiber

Pictured on page 17.

PINK MARGARITA SLUSH: Omit salt. Substitute sugar and coat rims as directed. Garnish with lemon wedges instead of lime wedges. Omit frozen limeade concentrate. Add 12½ oz. (355 mL) can of frozen concentrated cranberry lemonade, pink lemonade or cherry lemonade before blending.

Orange Milk Froth

Easy and quick.

Frozen concentrated orange juice	⅓ cup	75 mL
Milk	1 cup	250 mL
Ice cubes	3	3

Put all 3 ingredients into blender. Process until smooth. Serve immediately. Makes 2 cups (500 mL).

1 cup (250 mL): 133 Calories; 1.5 g Total Fat; 66 mg Sodium; 5 g Protein; 25 g Carbohydrate; trace Dietary Fiber

Blender

Italian-Type Dressing

This is one you will use often.

Light mayonnaise (not salad dressing)	1 cup	250 mL
Chopped onion	⅓ cup	75 mL
Red wine vinegar	2 tbsp.	30 mL
Dried whole oregano	½ tsp.	2 mL
Dried sweet basil	½ tsp.	2 mL
Granulated sugar	2 tbsp.	30 mL

Put all 6 ingredients into blender. Cover. Process until smooth. Makes 1½ cups (375 mL).

1 tbsp. (15 mL): 36 Calories; 3.1 g Total Fat; 67 mg Sodium; trace Protein; 2 g Carbohydrate; trace Dietary Fiber

Caesar Salad Dressing

Simple to make this popular dressing.

Large egg	1	1
Worcestershire sauce	1 tsp.	5 mL
Garlic powder	¼ tsp.	1 mL
Salt	½ tsp.	2 mL
Pepper	¼ tsp.	1 mL
Anchovy paste (optional)	2 tsp.	10 mL
Cooking oil	¾ cup	175 mL
Grated Parmesan cheese	¼ cup	60 mL
Lemon juice	3 tbsp.	50 mL

Put first 6 ingredients into blender. Process to mix.

With blender running, slowly drizzle in cooking oil.

Add cheese and lemon juice. Pulse with on/off motion 2 or 3 times. Makes 1⅓ cups (325 mL).

1 tbsp. (15 mL): 79 Calories; 8.4 g Total Fat; 89 mg Sodium; 1 g Protein; trace Carbohydrate; trace Dietary Fiber

Pictured on page 35 and on back cover (tossed with salad greens).

French-Type Dressing

Dress your tossed salad with this.

Can of condensed tomato soup	10 oz.	284 mL
Apple cider vinegar	¼ cup	60 mL
Cooking oil	3 tbsp.	50 mL
Chopped onion	⅓ cup	75 mL
Granulated sugar	¼ cup	60 mL
Worcestershire sauce	¾ tsp.	4 mL
Garlic powder	½ tsp.	2 mL
Salt	¼ tsp.	1 mL

Put all 8 ingredients into blender. Process until smooth. Makes 2 cups (500 mL).

1 tbsp. (15 mL): 24 Calories; 1.4 g Total Fat; 84 mg Sodium; trace Protein; 3 g Carbohydrate; trace Dietary Fiber

Pictured on page 35 and on back cover.

Blue Cheese Dressing

Good tangy blue flavor.

Light mayonnaise (not salad dressing)	1 cup	250 mL
Light sour cream	½ cup	125 mL
White vinegar	1 tbsp.	15 mL
Seasoned salt	1 tsp.	5 mL
Onion powder	¼ tsp.	1 mL
Garlic powder	¼ tsp.	1 mL
Salt	½ tsp.	2 mL
Pepper	¼ tsp.	1 mL
Crumbled blue cheese	¾ cup	175 mL
Milk (optional)	2 tbsp.	30 mL

Put first 9 ingredients into blender. Cover. Process until smooth. Add milk. Process just to blend. Makes 2 cups (500 mL).

1 tbsp. (15 mL): 38 Calories; 3.5 g Total Fat; 178 mg Sodium; 1 g Protein; 1 g Carbohydrate; trace Dietary Fiber

Mock Blue Cheese Mayo

Good dip for ribs, chicken wings and veggies.

Low-fat creamed cottage cheese	1 cup	250 mL
Water	2 tbsp.	30 mL
Lemon juice	2 tbsp.	30 mL
Skim milk powder	⅓ cup	75 mL
Seasoned salt	1 tsp.	5 mL
Onion powder	⅛ tsp.	0.5 mL
Crumbled blue cheese	2 tbsp.	30 mL

Put all 7 ingredients into blender. Process until smooth. Makes 1½ cups (375 mL).

2 tbsp. (30 mL): 33 Calories; 0.6 g Total Fat; 232 mg Sodium; 4 g Protein; 3 g Carbohydrate; trace Dietary Fiber

Mock Sour Cream

Ideal to use on baked potatoes, as a soup topping or where ever you want sour cream.

Low-fat creamed cottage cheese	1 cup	250 mL
Water	2 tbsp.	30 mL
Lemon juice	1 tbsp.	15 mL
Chopped chives (fresh is best)	1 tbsp.	15 mL

Put first 3 ingredients into blender. Process until smooth, scraping down sides if necessary, while processing. Turn into small bowl.

Add chives. Stir. Makes 1¼ cups (300 mL).

2 tbsp. (30 mL): 19 Calories; 0.3 g Total Fat; 104 mg Sodium; 3 g Protein; 1 g Carbohydrate; trace Dietary Fiber

Bread Machine

Take all the guesswork out of making aromatic loaves of bread with your bread machine! We tested these recipes using the 1½ pound (680 g)-capacity bread machine with eight settings: large light, large dark, regular light, french, sweet, quick bread, whole wheat and dough. Read your owner's manual to learn about your model's features and limitations. For best results, remove baked bread from pan immediately to avoid a soggy texture or collapsed top. If your bread machine also has a timer for delayed baking, any of our recipes, except those that contain dairy products, can be used following the manufacturer's instructions.

Panettone

Delicious bread has fruit well distributed throughout.

Water	¾ cup	175 mL
Hard margarine (or butter)	¼ cup	60 mL
Brown sugar, packed	¼ cup	60 mL
Aniseed, crushed	1 tsp.	5 mL
Salt	1½ tsp.	7 mL
Large eggs	2	2
Bread machine flour	3½ cups	875 mL
Bread machine yeast	1½ tsp.	7 mL
Raisins	¾ cup	175 mL
Glazed fruit	½ cup	125 mL
Grated lemon peel	2 tsp.	10 mL
Pine nuts	3 tbsp.	50 mL

Put first 8 ingredients into bread machine in order listed, making a small well in flour to hold yeast. Follow manufacturer's instructions.

Add raisins, glazed fruit, lemon peel and pine nuts at raisin/nut signal or about 5 minutes before last kneading is finished. Makes one 2¼ lb. (1 kg) loaf. Cuts into about 20 slices.

1 slice: 167 Calories; 4 g Total Fat; 244 mg Sodium; 4 g Protein; 30 g Carbohydrate; 1 g Dietary Fiber

Maple Wheat Bread

A nice syrupy sweetness in this loaf.

Warm water	¾ cup	175 mL
Maple syrup	⅓ cup	75 mL
Cooking oil	3 tbsp.	50 mL
Large egg	1	1
Salt	1½ tsp.	7 mL
Whole wheat flour	2 cups	500 mL
Bread flour	1½ cups	375 mL
Bread machine yeast	1½ tsp.	7 mL

Put all 8 ingredients into bread machine in order given, making a small well in flour to hold yeast. Follow manufacturer's instructions. Makes one 1½ lb. (680 g) loaf. Cuts into about 16 slices.

1 slice: 144 Calories; 3.3 g Total Fat; 260 mg Sodium; 4 g Protein; 26 g Carbohydrate; 2 g Dietary Fiber

Pictured on page 18.

Pumpernickel Bread

Good flavor and density.

Water	1¼ cups	300 mL
Fancy (mild) molasses	1 tbsp.	15 mL
Salt	1½ tsp.	7 mL
Cocoa	1 tbsp.	15 mL
Hard margarine (or butter)	1 tbsp.	15 mL
Potato flakes	⅓ cup	75 mL
All-bran cereal	¼ cup	60 mL
Bread flour	2¼ cups	550 mL
Rye flour	1 cup	250 mL
Bread machine yeast	1¾ tsp.	9 mL

Put all 10 ingredients into bread machine in order given, making a small well in flour to hold yeast. Follow manufacturer's instructions. Makes one 1½ lb. (680 g) loaf. Cuts into about 14 slices.

1 slice: 125 Calories; 1.3 g Total Fat; 314 mg Sodium; 3 g Protein; 25 g Carbohydrate; 3 g Dietary Fiber

Pictured on page 18.

Shredded Wheat Bread

A dense loaf with a pleasing flavor and texture.

Large shredded wheat biscuits, crumbled	1 cup	250 mL
Water	1¼ cups	300 mL
Fancy (mild) molasses	1½ tbsp.	25 mL
Cooking oil	2 tbsp.	30 mL
Salt	1 tsp.	5 mL
Brown sugar, packed	1½ tbsp.	25 mL
Wheat germ	3 tbsp.	50 mL
Bread flour	2¾ cups	675 mL
Bread machine yeast	1½ tsp.	7 mL

Put all 9 ingredients into bread machine into order given, making a small well in flour to hold yeast. Follow manufacturer's instructions. Makes one 1½ lb. (680 g) loaf. Cuts into about 16 slices.

1 slice: 134 Calories; 2.2 g Total Fat; 460 mg Sodium; 3 g Protein; 26 g Carbohydrate; 1 g Dietary Fiber

Oatmeal Bread

An even golden, crispy crust.

Water	1¼ cups	300 mL
Brown sugar, packed	2 tbsp.	30 mL
Cooking oil	2 tbsp.	30 mL
Salt	1½ tsp.	7 mL
Skim milk powder	⅓ cup	75 mL
Quick-cooking rolled oats	¾ cup	175 mL
Bread flour	3¼ cups	800 mL
Bread machine yeast	1¼ tsp.	6 mL

Put all 8 ingredients into bread machine in order given, making a small well in flour to hold yeast. Follow manufacturer's instructions. Makes one 1¾ lb. (790 g) loaf. Cuts into about about 16 slices.

1 slice: 145 Calories; 2.3 g Total Fat; 270 mg Sodium; 4 g Protein; 26 g Carbohydrate; 1 g Dietary Fiber

Bread Machine

Corn Bread

Nicely shaped full loaf. Not a sweet corn bread.

Milk	1 cup	250 mL
Large egg, fork-beaten	1	1
Hard margarine (or butter), melted	3 tbsp.	50 mL
Water	2 tbsp.	30 mL
Granulated sugar	1 tbsp.	15 mL
Salt	1½ tsp.	7 mL
Yellow cornmeal	½ cup	125 mL
Bread flour	3¼ cups	800 mL
Bread machine yeast	1¼ tsp.	6 mL

Put all 9 ingredients into bread machine in order given, making a small well in flour to hold yeast. Follow manufacturer's instructions. Makes one 1¾ lb. (790 g) loaf. Cuts into about 16 slices.

1 slice: 149 Calories; 3 g Total Fat; 293 mg Sodium; 4 g Protein; 26 g Carbohydrate; 1 g Dietary Fiber

Parmesan Bread

Savory Parmesan and oregano flavor in this large loaf.

Water	1⅓ cups	325 mL
Granulated sugar	2 tbsp.	30 mL
Skim milk powder	⅓ cup	75 mL
Cooking oil	2 tbsp.	30 mL
Seasoned salt	1½ tsp.	7 mL
Dried whole oregano	1½ -2 tsp.	7-10 mL
Onion powder	¼ tsp.	1 mL
Grated Parmesan cheese	⅓ cup	75 mL
Bread flour	3½ cups	875 mL
Bread machine yeast	1½ tsp.	7 mL

Put all 10 ingredients into bread machine in order given, making a small well in flour to hold yeast. Follow manufacturer's instructions. Makes one 1¾ lb. (790 g) loaf. Cuts into about 20 slices.

1 slice: 113 Calories; 2.2 g Total Fat; 146 mg Sodium; 4 g Protein; 19 g Carbohydrate; 1 g Dietary Fiber

Whole Wheat Bread

Whole wheat nutty flavor with a slight molasses sweetness.

Water	1½ cups	375 mL
Fancy (mild) molasses	2 tbsp.	30 mL
Brown sugar, packed	1½ tbsp.	25 mL
Cooking oil	2 tbsp.	30 mL
Salt	1½ tsp.	7 mL
Wheat germ	1 tbsp.	15 mL
Whole wheat flour	3¾ cups	925 mL
Bread machine yeast	1¾ tsp.	9 mL

Put all 8 ingredients into bread machine in order given, making a small well in flour to hold yeast. Follow manufacturer's instructions. Makes one 1 lb.10 oz. (740 g) loaf. Cuts into about 16 slices.

1 slice: 131 Calories; 2.3 g Total Fat; 257 mg Sodium; 4 g Protein; 25 g Carbohydrate; 4 g Dietary Fiber

Cracked Wheat Bread

Mellow nutty flavor. So good for sandwiches.

Fine cracked wheat	⅓ cup	75 mL
Boiling water	1 cup	250 mL
Milk	⅞ cup	200 mL
Granulated sugar	1½ tbsp.	25 mL
Fancy (mild) molasses	1½ tbsp.	25 mL
Hard margarine (or butter)	3 tbsp.	50 mL
Salt	1½ tsp.	7 mL
Whole wheat flour	1½ cup	325 mL
Bread flour	2½ cup	625 mL
Bread machine yeast	1½ tsp.	7 mL

Cook cracked wheat in boiling water in small saucepan until soft and mushy and most of liquid is absorbed. Turn into bread machine.

Add remaining 8 ingredients in order given, making a small well in flour to hold yeast. Follow manufacturer's instructions. Makes one 1¾ lb. (790 g) loaf. Cuts into about 16 slices.

1 slice: 161 Calories; 2.8 g Total Fat; 289 mg Sodium; 5 g Protein; 30 g Carbohydrate; 3 g Dietary Fiber

Orange Poppy Seed Bread

Wonderful orange flavor. Remember to use the 'Sweet' setting on your bread machine for this loaf.

Unsweetened prepared orange juice	1⅓ cups	325 mL
Skim milk powder	¼ cup	60 mL
Salt	1½ tsp.	7 mL
Liquid honey	2 tbsp.	30 mL
Poppy seeds	¼ cup	60 mL
Grated orange peel	2 tsp.	10 mL
Hard margarine (or butter), cut into 4 pieces	2 tbsp.	30 mL
Bread flour	3½ cups	875 mL
Bread machine yeast	1 tsp.	5 mL

Put all 9 ingredients into bread machine in order given, making a small well in flour to hold yeast. Follow manufacturer's instructions. Makes one 2 lb. (900 g) loaf. Cuts into about 20 slices.

1 slice: 125 Calories; 2.3 g Total Fat; 227 mg Sodium; 4 g Protein; 23 g Carbohydrate; 1 g Dietary Fiber

Pictured on page 18.

Honey Wheat Bread

Complement the nutty sweet flavor with some peanut butter for breakfast!

Milk	1 cup	250 mL
Water	¼ cup	60 mL
Liquid honey	¼ cup	60 mL
Hard margarine (or butter)	3 tbsp.	50 mL
Salt	1½ tsp.	7 mL
Bread flour	1¾ cups	425 mL
Whole wheat flour	2 cups	500 mL
Bread machine yeast	1½ tsp.	7 mL

Put all 8 ingredients into bread machine in order given, making a small well in flour to hold yeast. Follow manufacturer's instructions. Makes one 1½ lb. (680 g) loaf. Cuts into about 16 slices.

1 slice: 151 Calories; 2.8 g Total Fat; 290 mg Sodium; 4 g Protein; 28 g Carbohydrate; 3 g Dietary Fiber

Potato Bread

Simply the best bread ever.

Milk	½ cup	125 mL
Potato water	½ cup	125 mL
Mashed potato	½ cup	125 mL
Hard margarine (or butter)	3 tbsp.	50 mL
Granulated sugar	2 tbsp.	30 mL
Salt	1¼ tsp.	6 mL
Bread flour	3½ cups	875 mL
Bread machine yeast	1¼ tsp.	6 mL

Put all 8 ingredients into bread machine in order given, making a small well in flour to hold yeast. Follow manufacturer's instructions. Makes one 1½ lb. (680 g) loaf. Cuts into about 16 slices.

1 slice: 141 Calories; 2.6 g Total Fat; 243 mg Sodium; 4 g Protein; 26 g Carbohydrate; 1 g Dietary Fiber

Dill Bread

A slight tang from the yogurt goes so well with dill.

Plain yogurt	½ cup	125 mL
Cooking oil	1 tbsp.	15 mL
Water	¾ cup	175 mL
Granulated sugar	1 tbsp.	15 mL
Salt	1½ tsp.	7 mL
Dill weed (or seed)	1 tbsp.	15 mL
Bread flour	3¾ cups	925 mL
Bread machine yeast	1½ tsp.	7 mL

Put all 8 ingredients into bread machine in order given, making a small well in flour to hold yeast. Follow manufacturer's instructions. Makes one 1½ lb. (680 g) loaf. Cuts into about 16 slices.

1 slice: 131 Calories; 1.4 g Total Fat; 261 mg Sodium; 4 g Protein; 25 g Carbohydrate; 1 g Dietary Fiber

COTTAGE DILL BREAD: Omit yogurt. Add same amount of creamed cottage cheese plus 3 tbsp. (50 mL) water. Makes one 1½ lb. (680 g) loaf.

Pictured on page 35 and on back cover.

Bread Machine

Swedish Rye Bread

A light rye bread with a just a hint of anise or caraway.

Water	1⅛ cups	280 mL
Cooking oil	2 tbsp.	30 mL
Fancy (mild) molasses	2 tbsp.	30 mL
Aniseed (or caraway seed)	¾ tsp.	4 mL
Salt	1½ tsp.	7 mL
Rye flour	1 cup	250 mL
Bread flour	2½ cups	625 mL
Bread machine yeast	1½ tsp.	7 mL

Put all 8 ingredients into bread machine in order given, making a small well in flour to hold yeast. Follow manufacturer's instructions. Makes one 1½ lb. (680 g) loaf. Cuts into about 16 slices.

1 slice: 122 Calories; 2.1 g Total Fat; 256 mg Sodium; 3 g Protein; 23 g Carbohydrate; 2 g Dietary Fiber

Sally Lunn

Don't be fooled by the weight! This is a large, but light and airy loaf. Perfect for sandwiches or buttered toast.

Milk	1¼ cups	300 mL
Hard margarine (or butter), melted	6 tbsp.	100 mL
Large eggs	2	2
Granulated sugar	3 tbsp.	50 mL
Salt	1¼ tsp.	6 mL
Bread flour	3⅓ cups	825 mL
Bread machine yeast	1¼ tsp.	6 mL

Heat milk and margarine in small saucepan until melted. Pour into bread machine. Put remaining 5 ingredients into bread machine in order given, making a small well in flour to hold yeast. Follow manufacturer's instructions. Makes one 1¼ lb. (560 g) loaf. Cuts into about 16 slices.

1 slice: 164 Calories; 5.1 g Total Fat; 278 mg Sodium; 4 g Protein; 25 g Carbohydrate; 1 g Dietary Fiber

Cheese Bread

Crispy crust and very flavorful.

Milk	1 cup	250 mL
Water	⅓ cup	75 mL
Granulated sugar	2 tbsp.	30 mL
Hard margarine (or butter)	1 tbsp.	15 mL
Salt	1½ tsp.	7 mL
Grated Swiss cheese	1 cup	250 mL
Bread flour	3½ cups	875 mL
Bread machine yeast	1¼ tsp.	6 mL

Put all 8 ingredients into bread machine in order given, making a small well in flour to hold yeast. Follow manufacturer's instructions. Makes one 1¾ lb. (790 g) loaf. Cuts into about 16 slices.

1 slice: 152 Calories; 3.2 g Total Fat; 290 mg Sodium; 6 g Protein; 25 g Carbohydrate; 1 g Dietary Fiber

Herb Bread

A nice blend of herbs without being overpowering.

Water	1¼ cups	300 mL
Hard margarine (or butter)	2 tbsp.	30 mL
Granulated sugar	2 tbsp.	30 mL
Skim milk powder	3 tbsp.	50 mL
Dried whole oregano	½ tsp.	2 mL
Ground rosemary	½ tsp.	2 mL
Dried sweet basil	½ tsp.	2 mL
Parsley flakes	1 tsp.	5 mL
Dill weed	½ tsp.	2 mL
Grated Parmesan cheese	3 tbsp.	50 mL
Salt	1½ tsp.	7 mL
Bread flour	3¼ cups	800 mL
Bread machine yeast	1½ tsp.	7 mL

Put all 13 ingredients into bread machine in order given, making a small well in flour to hold yeast. Follow manufacturer's instructions. Makes one 1½ lb. (680 g) loaf. Cuts into 16 slices.

1 slice: 129 Calories; 2.1 g Total Fat; 302 mg Sodium; 4 g Protein; 23 g Carbohydrate; 1 g Dietary Fiber

Pictured on page 18.

Electric Frying Pan

 The model used for testing was a frying pan/griddle combination, with the temperature for the frying pan ranging from 200° to 400°F (95° to 205°C). Read your owner's manual to learn about your model's features and limitations. Most models have a non-stick surface, decreasing or even eliminating the need for added oil.

Curried Beef And Barley

Very mild curry flavor can be spiced up by adding more curry powder.

Cooking oil	1 tbsp.	15 mL
Beef round steak, cut into 1 inch (2.5 cm) cubes	1 lb.	454 g
Chopped onion	½ cup	125 mL
Garlic clove, minced	1	1
Seasoned salt	1 tsp.	5 mL
Curry powder	½ tsp.	2 mL
Cans of stewed tomatoes, with juice (14 oz., 398 mL, each)	2	2
Pot barley	¾ cup	175 mL
Water	1½ cups	375 mL
Dark raisins (optional)	⅓ cup	75 mL

Preheat non-stick electric frying pan to 400°F (205°C). Add cooking oil. Brown beef cubes. Add onion, garlic, seasoned salt and curry powder. Cook for about 2 minutes until onion is soft. Add stewed tomatoes, barley and water. Stir. Bring to a boil. Reduce heat to 250°F (120°C). Cover. Cook for 1 hour, stirring occasionally.

Add raisins. Cook for about 15 minutes, until barley is tender. Makes 5 cups (1.25 mL). Serves 4.

1 serving: 398 Calories; 10.2 g Total Fat; 958 mg Sodium; 32 g Protein; 47 g Carbohydrate; 9 g Dietary Fiber

Pictured on page 35 and on back cover.

Apricot Chicken

Baby carrots and white and wild rice complement this flavorful dish.

Cooking oil	1 tbsp.	15 mL
Boneless, skinless chicken breast halves (about 1 lb., 454 g)	4	4
Milk	1¾ cups	425 mL
All-purpose flour	1 tbsp.	15 mL
Chopped dried apricots	½ cup	125 mL
Green onions, sliced	3	3
Ground ginger	¼ tsp.	1 mL
Paprika	¼ tsp.	1 mL
Chicken bouillon powder	2 tsp.	10 mL

Preheat non-stick electric frying pan to 400°F (205°C). Add cooking oil. Brown chicken quickly on both sides. Remove to plate. Reduce heat to 325°F (160°C).

Gradually whisk milk into flour in small bowl until smooth. Pour milk mixture into frying pan. Cook and stir until boiling and thickened.

Stir in remaining 5 ingredients. Add chicken. Cover. Cook slowly for about 20 minutes until no pink remains in chicken. Serves 4.

1 serving: 318 Calories; 7.1 g Total Fat; 492 mg Sodium; 44 g Protein; 18 g Carbohydrate; 2 g Dietary Fiber

Pictured on page 36.

1. Cottage Dill Bread, page 30 **(Bread Machine)**
2. Caesar Salad Dressing, page 21 (shown on salad) **(Blender)**
3. Curried Beef And Barley, page 33 **(Electric Frying Pan)**
4. Boston Brown Bread, page 122 **(Slow Cooker)**
5. French-Type Dressing, page 22 **(Blender)**

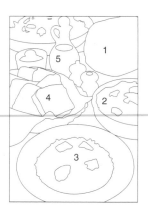

Electric Frying Pan

Chicken Peking

The sauce makes this outstanding. Toasted sesame seeds make a nice garnish.

Cooking oil	1 tbsp.	15 mL
Boneless, skinless chicken breast halves	4	4
(about 1 lb., 454 g)		
Chopped onion	1 cup	250 mL
Finely chopped gingerroot	1½ tbsp.	25 mL
Finely chopped garlic	2 tsp.	10 mL
Teriyaki sauce	⅓ cup	75 mL
Lemon juice	2 tbsp.	30 mL

Preheat non-stick electric frying pan to 350°F (175°C). Add cooking oil. Sauté chicken, onion, gingerroot and garlic until browned. Reduce heat to 250°F (120°C).

Stir teriyaki sauce and lemon juice in small bowl. Pour over chicken mixture. Cover. Simmer for 15 to 20 minutes until tender, turning chicken after 8 minutes and adding more water if needed. Serves 4.

1 serving: 218 Calories; 5.4 g Total Fat; 513 mg Sodium; 33 g Protein; 8 g Carbohydrate; 1 g Dietary Fiber

1. Shrimp Cantonese, page 44
   (Electric Frying Pan)
2. Tartar Sauce, page 48
   (Food Processor)
3. Apricot Chicken, page 34
   (Electric Frying Pan)
4. Poached Salmon, page 44
   (Electric Frying Pan)

Props Courtesy Of: Le Gnome
Winners Stores

Chicken Stew

Although you can make this without dumplings, they do add the finishing touch.

Cooking oil	1 tbsp.	15 mL
Chicken thighs (about 3 lbs., 1.4 kg), skin removed	12	12
Medium onions, cut up	2	2
Water	3 cups	750 mL
Chicken bouillon powder	1 tbsp.	15 mL
Vegetable bouillon powder	1 tbsp.	15 mL
Pepper	¼ tsp.	1 mL
Medium carrots, cut into ½ inch (12 mm) slices	4	4
Medium potatoes, cubed	4	4
Cubed yellow turnip	2 cups	500 mL
Cornstarch	2 tbsp.	30 mL
Water	2 tbsp.	30 mL
Frozen green beans	1 cup	250 mL
DUMPLINGS		
All-purpose flour	1½ cups	375 mL
Baking powder	1 tbsp.	15 mL
Granulated sugar	1½ tsp.	7 mL
Salt	¾ tsp.	4 mL
Cooking oil	1½ tbsp.	25 mL
Milk	¾ cup	175 mL

Preheat non-stick electric frying pan to 375°F (190°C). Add cooking oil. Sauté chicken and onion until chicken is browned and onion is soft.

Add water, both bouillon powders and pepper. Stir around chicken to blend spices. Add carrot, potato and turnip. Reduce heat to 275°F (140°C). Cover. Simmer for about 45 minutes until chicken is no longer pink and vegetables are tender.

Stir cornstarch and water in small cup. Stir into chicken mixture until boiling and thickened.

(continued on next page)

Electric Frying Pan

Add green beans. Stir lightly to ensure beans are underneath other vegetables.

Dumplings: Stir first 4 ingredients in medium bowl. Add cooking oil and milk. Stir to moisten. Drop by heaping spoonfuls in about 12 dabs over stew and simmering liquid. Cover. Keep liquid boiling for about 12 minutes. Do not lift cover. Serves 6.

1 serving: 483 Calories; 12.4 g Total Fat; 1149 mg Sodium; 35 g Protein; 57 g Carbohydrate; 5 g Dietary Fiber

Chicken Mornay

There's enough of this favorite sauce to serve over pasta, potatoes or even rice.

Cooking oil	1 tbsp.	15 mL
Boneless, skinless chicken breast halves	6	6
(about 1½ lbs., 680 g)		
MORNAY SAUCE		
Can of skim evaporated milk	13½ oz.	385 mL
All-purpose flour	¼ cup	60 mL
Salt	½ tsp.	2 mL
Pepper	⅛ tsp.	0.5 mL
Chicken bouillon powder	1 tsp.	5 mL
Grated Parmesan cheese	¼ cup	60 mL
Grated Swiss cheese	½ cup	125 mL
Milk	¾ cup	175 mL

Preheat non-stick electric frying pan to 375°F (190°C). Add cooking oil. Brown chicken breasts on both sides. Transfer to plate. Reduce heat to 325°F (160°C).

Mornay Sauce: Gradually whisk evaporated milk into flour in small bowl until smooth. Pour into frying pan. Heat and stir until boiling and thickened.

Stir in remaining 6 ingredients. Makes 1¾ cups (425 mL) sauce.

Add chicken. Spoon sauce over top to coat. Cover. Cook for about 15 minutes until chicken is no longer pink. Serves 6.

1 serving: 331 Calories; 8.7 g Total Fat; 635 mg Sodium; 46 g Protein; 14 g Carbohydrate; trace Dietary Fiber

Pineapple Chicken

Tender chicken and delicious sauce to serve over rice.

Garlic salt	¼ tsp.	1 mL
Celery salt	¼ tsp.	1 mL
Seasoned salt	¼ tsp.	1 mL
Ground nutmeg	¼ tsp.	1 mL
Paprika	¼ tsp.	1 mL
Cooking oil	2 tbsp.	30 mL
Chicken parts, skin removed	4 lbs.	1.8 kg
Can of crushed pineapple, drained and juice reserved	14 oz.	398 mL
Chopped onion	½ cup	125 mL
All-purpose flour	2 tbsp.	30 mL
Brown sugar, packed	2 tbsp.	30 mL
Soy sauce	3 tbsp.	50 mL
Reserved pineapple juice plus water to equal	1 cup	250 mL
Ketchup	1 tbsp.	15 mL

Stir first 5 ingredients in small cup.

Preheat non-stick electric frying pan to 375°F (190°C). Add cooking oil. Brown chicken parts. Sprinkle with seasonings while browning.

Scatter pineapple and onion over chicken. Cover. Reduce heat to 300°F (150°C). Cook for 40 minutes. Remove chicken to platter. Cover to keep warm.

Combine flour and brown sugar in small bowl. Stir in soy sauce, juice mixture and ketchup until smooth. Add to pan. Stir until boiling and thickened. Pour over chicken. Serves 6.

1 serving: 297 Calories; 9 g Total Fat; 838 mg Sodium; 33 g Protein; 20 g Carbohydrate; 1 g Dietary Fiber

 tip
Save time making your favorite loaf in the bread machine by mixing up several batches of the dry ingredients, excluding the yeast. Store each batch in an airtight container or resealable freezer bag and place in the cupboard. When it's time for steaming, hot bread, just add the wet ingredients, then the pre-mixed dry, then the yeast.

Chicken Fried Rice

A nice combination of flavors. Good choice.

Cooking oil	2 tsp.	10 mL
Boneless, skinless chicken breast halves, (about 3), cut into ¾ inch (2 cm) cubes	¾ lb.	340 g
Medium onion, chopped	1	1
Thinly sliced celery	½ cup	125 mL
Finely chopped garlic	1 tsp.	5 mL
Gingerroot slice (⅛ inch, 3 mm, piece)	1	1
Water	1¾ cups	425 mL
Chicken bouillon powder	2 tsp.	10 mL
Long grain white rice	1 cup	250 mL
Large eggs	2	2
Soy sauce	1½ tbsp.	25 mL
Thinly sliced green onion	2 tbsp.	30 mL

Preheat non-stick electric frying pan to 375°F (190°C). Add cooking oil. Sauté chicken, first amount of onion, celery, garlic and gingerroot until browned. Reduce heat to 275°F (140°C).

Add water, bouillon powder and rice. Stir. Cover. Simmer for 25 to 30 minutes until rice is tender. Discard gingerroot. Make well in center. Increase heat to 325°F (160°C).

Beat eggs and soy sauce in small bowl. Stir in green onion. Pour into well in rice. Cook and stir just in the well for about 3 minutes until set. Combine with rice. Makes 5 cups (1.25 L). Serves 4.

1 serving: 357 Calories; 6.5 g Total Fat; 813 mg Sodium; 28 g Protein; 45 g Carbohydrate; 2 g Dietary Fiber

Variation: For added color, include cooked diced carrot or peas, or both.

Paré Pointer
Two wrongs never make a right but
two Wrights made an airplane.

Turkey Patties

Which one to try first — the variations are so good as well.

Large egg, fork-beaten	1	1
Milk	¼ cup	60 mL
Fine dry bread crumbs	½ cup	125 mL
Chicken (or vegetable) bouillon powder	2 tsp.	10 mL
Salt	½ tsp.	2 mL
Pepper	¼ tsp.	1 mL
Ground turkey	1½ lbs.	680 g
Large eggs	2	2
Water	1 tbsp.	15 mL
Cooking oil	1 tbsp.	15 mL
Fine dry bread crumbs	½ cup	125 mL

Combine first 6 ingredients in large bowl.

Add ground turkey. Mix well. Shape into 12 patties.

Beat eggs and water together with fork in small bowl.

Preheat non-stick electric frying pan to 350°F (175°C). Add cooking oil. Dip patties into egg mixture. Coat with bread crumbs. Brown well for about 5 minutes per side until cooked. Makes 12 small patties.

2 patties: 265 Calories; 7.8 g Total Fat; 690 mg Sodium; 31 g Protein; 15 g Carbohydrate; trace Dietary Fiber

Variation: To crumbs, add ¾ cup (175 mL) grated Monterey Jack cheese, ¾ tsp. (4 mL) chili powder and 3 tbsp. (50 mL) chopped jalapeño or hot peppers (see Tip, page 49).

Variation: To crumbs, add 1½ tsp. (7 mL) no-salt garlic herb seasoning and 1½ tsp. (7 mL) parley flakes.

CHICKEN PATTIES: Substitute ground chicken for ground turkey.

Turkey Stroganoff

No one can tell you have used fat-free sour cream in this.
Stroganoff doesn't always have to be beef.

Cooking oil	1 tbsp.	15 mL
Diced boneless, skinless turkey	4 cups	1 L
Medium onion, chopped	1	1
Sliced fresh mushrooms	1 cup	250 mL
All-purpose flour	¼ cup	60 mL
Chicken bouillon powder	1 tbsp.	15 mL
Salt	¼ tsp.	1 mL
Pepper	¼ tsp.	1 mL
Ground marjoram	⅛ tsp.	0.5 mL
Water	2 cups	500 mL
Ketchup	2 tbsp.	30 mL
Non-fat sour cream	1 cup	250 mL
White vinegar	2 tsp.	10 mL

Preheat non-stick electric frying pan to 350°F (175°C). Add cooking oil. Add turkey and onion. Sauté until turkey is browned and onion is soft.

Add mushrooms. Sauté about 14 minutes until turkey is cooked and moisture is evaporated.

Sprinkle flour, bouillon powder, salt, pepper and marjoram over top. Mix well. Stir in water and ketchup until boiling and thickened.

Combine sour cream and vinegar in small bowl. Add to turkey mixture. Stir to heat through (do not boil). Makes 6 cups (1.5 L). Serves 4 to 6.

1 serving: 319 Calories; 7.1 g Total Fat; 905 mg Sodium; 47 g Protein; 15 g Carbohydrate; 1 g Dietary Fiber

 When making bread or cracker crumbs in the blender or food processor, tear or break the bread slices into pieces first. You may prefer to remove crusts on fresh bread slices as they are difficult to process to the crumb stage.

Poached Salmon

A delicate flavor to this favorite fish. Extra healthy when poached.

Water	1 cup	250 mL
Vegetable (or chicken) bouillon powder	1½ tsp.	7 mL
Apple juice	⅓ cup	75 mL
Lime (or lemon) juice	2 tsp.	10 mL
Salmon fillets or steaks (about 1 lb., 454 g)	4	4
Fresh dill, for garnish		

Combine water, bouillon powder, apple juice and lime juice in non-stick electric frying pan. Bring to a boil at 350°F (175°C).

Measure thickest part of salmon. Add to pan. Return to gentle boil. Cover. Poach for 10 minutes per 1 inch (2.5 cm) thickness until fish flakes when tested with fork. Remove to serving platter.

Garnish with fresh dill. Makes 4 servings.

1 serving: 152 Calories; 5.4 g Total Fat; 331 mg Sodium; 23 g Protein; 3 g Carbohydrate; trace Dietary Fiber

Pictured on page 36.

Glazed Ham Slice

A simple way to dress up ham.

No-stick cooking spray		
Thick ham steaks, trimmed of fat (see Note)	1½ lbs.	680 g
Cranberry jelly	½ cup	125 mL
Prepared orange juice	2 tbsp.	30 mL
Brown sugar, packed	½ tbsp.	7 mL
White vinegar	1 tbsp.	15 mL
Ground cloves	¹⁄₁₆ tsp.	0.5 mL

Spray non-stick electric frying pan with no-stick cooking spray. Preheat to 350° to 400°F (175° to 205°C). Lightly brown ham steaks on both sides.

(continued on next page)

Electric Frying Pan

Mix cranberry jelly, orange juice, brown sugar, vinegar and cloves in small bowl. Spread over ham. Simmer for about 2 minutes. Turn. Simmer for about 2 minutes. Cut into serving size pieces. Serves 6.

1 serving: 182 Calories; 4.9 g Total Fat; 1446 mg Sodium; 22 g Protein; 11 g Carbohydrate; trace Dietary Fiber

Note: Boneless ham yields 6 servings. You will need slightly more weight if it contains bone.

Shrimp Cantonese

Serve over plenty of hot, fluffy rice.

Cooking oil	2 tbsp.	30 mL
Medium onion, sliced lengthwise in wedges	1	1
Thinly sliced celery, on the diagonal	2 cups	500 mL
Small red or green pepper, slivered	1	1
Can of bamboo shoots, drained	8 oz.	227 mL
Can of sliced water chestnuts, drained	8 oz.	227 mL
Bean sprouts	2 cups	500 mL
Coarsely chopped fresh spinach, lightly packed	2 cups	500 mL
SAUCE		
Can of condensed chicken broth	10 oz.	284 mL
Soy sauce	¼ cup	60 mL
Cornstarch	2 tbsp.	30 mL
Ground ginger	⅛ tsp.	0.5 mL
Pepper	⅛ tsp.	0.5 mL
Cooked medium shrimp	10 oz.	285 g

Preheat non-stick electric frying pan to 375°F (190°C). Add cooking oil. Sauté onion, celery and pepper slivers for 2 to 3 minutes until starting to soften. Add bamboo shoots, water chestnuts, bean sprouts and spinach. Stir well. Cover. Cook for 5 minutes until spinach is soft.

Sauce: Combine first 5 ingredients in small bowl. Add to frying pan. Stir to combine. Reduce heat to 325°F (160°C).

Scatter shrimp over top of vegetables. Cover. Cook for 5 minutes until boiling and thickened and shrimp are hot. Makes 7 cups (1.75 L).

1 cup (250 mL): 147 Calories; 5.1 g Total Fat; 1035 mg Sodium; 13 g Protein; 13 g Carbohydrate; 2 g Dietary Fiber

Pictured on page 36.

Sweet and Sour Ribs

Lots of tasty sauce for rice. This is a perfect make-ahead recipe. Cook completely the day before. Chill and discard hardened fat from the surface before reheating. This will eliminate a lot of the saturated fat.

Cooking oil	1 tbsp.	15 mL
Sweet and sour spareribs, cut into 1-rib pieces	4 lbs.	1.8 kg
Paprika	1½ tsp.	7 mL
Salt	1 tsp.	5 mL
Pepper	½ tsp.	2 mL
Water	2 cups	500 mL
Cornstarch	2 tbsp.	30 mL
Apple cider vinegar	¼ cup	60 mL
Worcestershire sauce	2 tbsp.	30 mL
Brown sugar, packed	½ cup	125 mL
Soy sauce	3 tbsp.	50 mL
Ketchup	2 tbsp.	30 mL

Preheat non-stick electric frying pan to 400°F (205°C). Add cooking oil. Add ribs. Sprinkle with paprika, salt and pepper. Cook in 2 batches, turning frequently, until well browned. Reduce heat to 250°F (120°C).

Whisk remaining 7 ingredients in medium bowl. Pour over ribs. Stir until boiling and thickened slightly. Cover. Cook for about 1½ hours until ribs are very tender. Serves 6.

1 serving: 748 Calories; 56.3 g Total Fat; 1261 mg Sodium; 34 g Protein; 25 g Carbohydrate; trace Dietary Fiber

---

Paré Pointer
To make a child's pants last, make the shirt first.

Cranberry-Glazed Chops

Richly colored and very good.

All-purpose flour	¼ cup	60 mL
Ground ginger	1 tsp.	5 mL
Paprika	1 tsp.	5 mL
Salt	½ tsp.	2 mL
Pepper	¼ tsp.	1 mL
Cooking oil	1 tbsp.	15 mL
Bone-in pork loin chops (about 2 lbs., 900 g), trimmed of fat, cut ½ inch (12 mm) thick	6	6
Brown sugar, packed	⅓ cup	75 mL
Apple cider vinegar	⅓ cup	75 mL
Cranberry sauce	14 oz.	398 mL

Combine first 5 ingredients on a sheet of wax paper.

Preheat non-stick electric frying pan to 400°F (205°C). Add cooking oil. Dredge pork chops in flour mixture. Fry chops until browned. Reduce heat to 275°F (140°C). Arrange chops in a single layer.

Sprinkle surface of chops with brown sugar and then vinegar. Stir the cranberry sauce to break up. Spoon over chops. Cover. Cook for 20 minutes. Turn chops. Stir sauce and spoon some over chops. Cover. Cook for 20 minutes until chops are tender. Serves 6.

1 serving: 353 Calories; 8.2 g Total Fat; 314 mg Sodium; 22 g Protein; 48 g Carbohydrate; 1 g Dietary Fiber

 When using a hand blender, you will get better results and have less chance of a spillover if you use a tall, deep container. Many hand blenders come with their own cylinder or beaker.

Food Processor

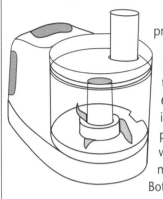

In addition to mixing, grating and puréeing, food processors shred, slice and mix. Read your owner's manual to learn about your model's features and limitations. Some of the following recipes were tested with a food processor with a capacity for 6 cups (1.5 L) dry or 2 cups (500 mL) wet ingredients. It had high and low speeds as well as pulse and continuous modes. Some of our recipes were also tested with a 3¼ cup (800 mL) capacity model which had only pulse and continuous mode. Both had grater and slicer attachments.

Tartar Sauce

A great tangy sauce to use with fish, tuna salad sandwiches and fish burgers.

Light salad dressing (or mayonnaise)	1 cup	250 mL
Baby dill pickles	6	6
Dill pickle juice	1 tbsp.	15 mL
Granulated sugar	1 tsp.	5 mL
Onion powder	¼ tsp.	1 mL
Parsley flakes	¼ tsp.	1 mL

Secure knife blade in food processor. Add all 6 ingredients. Cover. Pulse with on/off motion 18 to 20 times until pickle is finely chopped but not puréed. Makes 1⅔ cups (400 mL).

2 tbsp. (30 mL): 55 Calories; 4.6 g Total Fat; 245 mg Sodium; trace Protein; 3 g Carbohydrate; trace Dietary Fiber

Pictured on page 36.

Quick Salsa

Instead of tediously cutting all these vegetables by hand, use your food processor. Serve this colorful salsa with an assortment of tortilla chips.

Small garlic clove	1	1
Jalapeño pepper, halved and seeded (see Tip, below)	1	1
Green or yellow pepper, cut into chunks	½	½
Medium red onion, cut into chunks	½	½
Medium roma (plum) tomatoes (about 1 lb., 454 g), quartered	6	6
Fresh cilantro, to taste (optional)		
Salt	½ tsp.	2 mL
Ground cumin	⅛ tsp.	0.5 mL
Freshly ground pepper, sprinkle		
Can of chopped green chilies, drained	4 oz.	114 g
Lime juice	2 tsp.	10 mL

Secure knife blade in processor bowl. With processor running, drop garlic clove and jalapeño pepper through feed chute. Turn off.

Remove lid. Add pepper and red onion to processor bowl. Secure lid. Pulse with on/off motion 8 to 10 times until coarsely diced. Scrape down processor bowl with spatula.

Add tomato, cilantro, salt, cumin and pepper. Secure lid. Pulse several times. Scrape sides down. Pulse several times until salsa is desired texture. Empty into container.

Stir in green chilies and lime juice. Let stand at room temperature for 1 hour to blend flavors. Can be stored covered in refrigerator for up to 1 week. Makes 3½ cups (875 mL).

2 tbsp. (30 mL): 5 Calories; 0.1 g Total Fat; 71 mg Sodium; trace Protein; 1 g Carbohydrate; trace Dietary Fiber

Pictured on page 54.

 Wear protective gloves when handling jalapeño peppers. Do not touch your face near eyes.

Potato Salad

Finely chopped salad makes good use of the processor at every stage.

Medium waxy potatoes, with peel (about 3), quartered	1¼ lbs.	560 g
Water		
Hard-boiled eggs, peeled and halved	3	3
DRESSING		
Green onions, cut into 4 pieces each	3	3
Light salad dressing (or mayonnaise)	½ cup	125 mL
White vinegar	1 tbsp.	15 mL
Dry mustard	¼ tsp.	1 mL
Milk	1 tbsp.	15 mL
Salt	½ tsp.	2 mL
Pepper	⅛ tsp.	0.5 mL
Small head of iceberg lettuce, cut into wedges	½	½

Cook potatoes in water in medium saucepan until tender. Drain. Rinse with cold water. Drain. Cool thoroughly. Peel off skins. Secure knife blade in processor bowl. Add potatoes in small batches. Cover. Pulse with on/off motion until coarsely chopped. Turn into large bowl. Repeat until all potato is chopped.

Put egg halves into processor. Pulse until coarsely chopped. Empty into bowl with potatoes.

Dressing: Put dressing ingredients into processor. Pulse to mix. Scrape into bowl with potatoes.

Put lettuce into processor. Pulse until chopped. Add to bowl. Toss to combine. Makes 4 cups (1 L).

¼ cup (175 mL): 165 Calories; 7.3 g Total Fat; 382 mg Sodium; 5 g Protein; 21 g Carbohydrate; 2 g Dietary Fiber

 To get nice even slices when using the slicer attachment in the food processor, push the food straight down the feed chute, with a light steady pressure.

Mixed Slaw

Lots of crunchy satisfaction in this salad.

SALAD

Small head of cabbage, cut into wedges	½	½
Small head of iceberg lettuce, cut into wedges	½	½
English cucumber, cut into pieces	½	½
Small radishes	8	8
Green onions, cut into 1 inch (2.5 cm) pieces	2	2

DRESSING

Light salad dressing (or mayonnaise)	¼ cup	60 mL
Light sour cream	2 tbsp.	30 mL
Granulated sugar	1 tsp.	5 mL
Cooking oil	1 tsp.	5 mL
Salt	¼ tsp.	1 mL
Pepper	¹⁄₁₆ tsp.	0.5 mL
Dill weed	½ tsp.	2 mL

Salad: Secure slicer disc in processor bowl. Cover. Push cabbage through chute to slice. Empty into large bowl as processor bowl fills. Repeat with lettuce, cucumber and radish. Add to cabbage as processor bowl fills.

Change slicer disc to knife blade. Cover. Put green onion into processor through chute. Pulse with on/off motion until finely chopped. Add to cabbage.

Dressing: Mix all 7 ingredients, either in food processor fitted with knife blade, or in small bowl. Makes ⅓ cup (75 mL) dressing. Just before serving pour over salad. Toss to coat. Makes 9 cups (2.25 L).

1 cup (250 mL): 57 Calories; 2.8 g Total Fat; 150 mg Sodium; 2 g Protein; 8 g Carbohydrate; 2 g Dietary Fiber

Pictured on page 53.

Paré Pointer

When a health food salesman comes to your door, be sure to vitamin.

Coleslaw

This is the easiest way to make a tasty cabbage salad.

SALAD

Small head of cabbage, cut into wedges	½	½
Medium carrot, cut into pieces	1	1
Small red onion, cut into wedges	1	1
English cucumber, cut into pieces	½	½

DRESSING

Salad dressing (or mayonnaise)	⅓ cup	75 mL
White vinegar	4 tsp.	20 mL
Milk	2 tbsp.	30 mL
Granulated sugar	3 tbsp.	50 mL
Onion powder	¼ tsp.	1 mL
Paprika	¼ tsp.	1 mL
Salt	½ tsp.	2 mL
Pepper	⅛ tsp.	0.5 mL

Salad: Cut vegetables to fit feed chute. Secure slicer disc in food processor. Push cabbage through chute to slice. Empty into large bowl as processor bowl fills. Change slicer disc to shredding disc. Shred carrot, onion and cucumber. Add to cabbage. Stir. Chill until serving time.

Dressing: Mix all 8 ingredients in small bowl. Makes ⅔ cup (150 mL) dressing. Several hours before serving, stir dressing into cabbage mixture. Chill. Makes 6 cups (1.5 L).

½ cup (125 mL): 68 Calories; 3.5 g Total Fat; 170 mg Sodium; 1 g Protein; 9 g Carbohydrate; 1 g Dietary Fiber

1. Whole Wheat Twists, page 58
   (Food Processor)
2. Mixed Slaw, page 51
   (Food Processor)
3. Cheese Gnocchi, page 60
   (Food Processor)
4. Pizza Wheat Crust, page 57
   (with your choice of toppings)
   (Food Processor)

Props Courtesy Of: Stokes

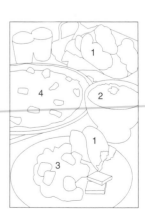

Food Processor

Biscuit Pizza Crust

The quickest crust going. No rising needed.

All-purpose flour	2 cups	500 mL
Baking powder	1 tbsp.	15 mL
Cold hard margarine (or butter)	2 tbsp.	30 mL
Salt	¼ tsp.	1 mL
Cold water	⅔ cup	150 mL

Secure knife blade in food processor. Add flour, baking powder, margarine and salt. Cover. Pulse with on/off motion about 6 times to cut up margarine.

With machine running, pour water through feed chute. Process for 50 to 60 seconds until dough forms a ball. Roll out on lightly floured surface. Press in greased 12 inch (30 cm) pizza pan, forming rim around edge. Top with pizza ingredients. Bake on bottom rack in 425°F (220°C) oven for 12 to 14 minutes. Cuts into 8 wedges.

1 wedge: 149 Calories; 3.3 g Total Fat; 126 mg Sodium; 3 g Protein; 26 g Carbohydrate; 1 g Dietary Fiber

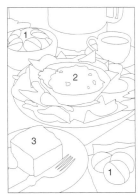

1. Shortbread, page 62 **(Food Processor)**
2. Quick Salsa, page 49 **(Food Processor)**
3. White Cake, page 63 **(Food Processor)** with Chocolate Icing, page 77 **(Hand Blender)**

Props Courtesy Of: Le Gnome

Pizza Crust

A yeasty crust that can be used immediately
or you can choose to let it rise once before using.

All-purpose flour	2 cups	500 mL
Instant yeast	1½ tsp.	7 mL
Salt	¼ tsp.	1 mL
Very warm water	⅔ cup	150 mL
Cooking oil	1 tbsp.	15 mL

Secure knife blade in food processor. Add flour, yeast and salt. Cover.

With machine running, pour water and cooking oil through feed chute. Process for 50 to 60 seconds until dough forms a ball. For a thicker crust, let dough rise in large greased bowl, turning once to grease top. Cover with tea towel. Let stand in oven with light on and door closed for about 1 hour until doubled in bulk. Punch dough down. Roll out on lightly floured surface and press in greased 12 inch (30 cm) pizza pan, forming rim around edge. Top with pizza ingredients. Bake on bottom rack in 425°F (220°C) oven for about 15 minutes. Cuts into 8 wedges.

1 wedge: 138 Calories; 2.1 g Total Fat; 86 mg Sodium; 4 g Protein; 25 g Carbohydrate; 1 g Dietary Fiber

THIN PIZZA CRUST: Reduce flour to 1½ cups (375 mL). Reduce water to ½ cup (125 mL). Crust will cook in 2 to 3 minutes less time.

 For cleaner slices of food with peel or skin, such as apples, push pieces into food processor feed chute so peel faces center of bowl.

Pizza Wheat Crust

Slightly heavier dough with whole wheat flour. Tasty.

Whole wheat flour	1¼ cups	300 mL
All-purpose flour	¾ cup	175 mL
Instant yeast	1½ tsp.	7 mL
Salt	¼ tsp.	1 mL
Very warm water	¾ cup	175 mL
Cooking oil	1½ tbsp.	25 mL

Secure knife blade in food processor. Add both flours, yeast and salt. Cover.

With machine running, pour water and cooking oil through feed chute. Process for 50 to 60 seconds until dough forms a ball. For a thicker crust, let dough rise in large greased bowl, turning once to grease top. Cover with tea towel. Let stand in oven with light on and door closed for about 1 hour until doubled in bulk. Punch dough down. Roll out on lightly floured surface. Press in greased 12 inch (30 cm) pizza pan, forming rim around edge. Top with pizza ingredients. Bake on bottom rack in 425°F (220°C) oven for about 15 minutes. Cuts into 8 wedges.

1 wedge: 137 Calories; 3 g Total Fat; 86 mg Sodium; 4 g Protein; 24 g Carbohydrate; 3 g Dietary Fiber

Pictured on page 57.

Paré Pointer

He stole not only money but all kinds of jewelry as well.
He knew that money alone doesn't buy happiness.

Whole Wheat Twists

*A small treat for a small family. This recipe uses both
the food processor and toaster oven.*

Warm water	⅓ cup	75 mL
Granulated sugar	1½ tsp.	7 mL
Active dry yeast	1¼ tsp.	6 mL
Very warm milk	⅓ cup	75 mL
Hard margarine (or butter)	2 tbsp.	30 mL
Fancy (mild) molasses	1 tbsp.	15 mL
Salt	¾ tsp.	4 mL
Whole wheat flour	1 cup	250 mL
All-purpose flour	1 cup	250 mL

Stir water and sugar in small bowl. Sprinkle yeast over top. Let stand for 10 minutes. Stir to dissolve.

Measure milk, margarine, molasses and salt into small bowl. Add yeast mixture. Stir.

Secure knife blade in food processor. Add both flours. Cover. With machine running, pour yeast mixture through feed chute. Process for 50 to 60 seconds until dough forms a ball. Place dough in greased bowl, turning once to grease top. Cover with tea towel. Let stand in oven with light on and door closed for 1 to 1½ hours until doubled in bulk. Punch dough down. Divide into 6 equal portions. Divide each portion into 2 pieces. Roll each into 7 inch (18 cm) rope. Join 2 ropes at each end. Twist one end over 3 times. Arrange on greased baking sheet that comes with toaster oven. Cover with tea towel. Let stand in oven with door closed and light on for about 45 minutes until doubled in size. Bake in preheated toaster oven at 350°F (175°C) for 13 to 15 minutes. Transfer to racks to cool. Makes 6 twists.

1 twist: 208 Calories; 4.7 g Total Fat; 395 mg Sodium; 6 g Protein; 36 g Carbohydrate; 4 g Dietary Fiber

Pictured on page 53.

Scalloped Potatoes

This version has a delicious cheesy onion sauce. Very good.

Medium potatoes	6	6
Large onion	1	1
Light sharp Cheddar cheese	4 oz.	113 g
SAUCE		
All-purpose flour	¼ cup	60 mL
Salt	1½ tsp.	7 mL
Pepper	¼ tsp.	1 mL
Paprika	¼ tsp.	1 mL
Milk	1 cup	250 mL
Skim evaporated milk (or milk)	1 cup	250 mL

Cut potatoes, onion and cheese to fit feed chute. Secure slicer disc in food processor. Cover. Push potatoes through chute to slice. Transfer to bowl. Slice onion. Transfer to separate bowl.

Change slicer disc to shredder disc. Cover. Put cheese through chute to grate. Place alternate layers of potato, onion and cheese in greased 2 quart (2 L) casserole.

Sauce: Mix flour, salt, pepper and paprika in medium saucepan. Gradually whisk in both milks until smooth. Heat and stir until boiling and thickened. Pour over casserole. Poke here and there to allow sauce to run into casserole. Cover. Bake in 350°F (175°C) oven for 60 minutes. Remove cover. Bake for 15 minutes until potatoes are tender. Serves 6.

1 serving: 229 Calories; 4.5 g Total Fat; 880 mg Sodium; 13 g Protein; 34 g Carbohydrate; 2 g Dietary Fiber

 Save vegetable pulp from the juicer to make soup. The pulp may be frozen or used immediately.

Cheese Gnocchi

Delicious sauce over chewy pasta.

GNOCCHI

Medium baking potato, with peel (about 6 to 8 oz., 170 to 225 g)	1	1
Water	1 cup	250 g
Salt	¼ tsp.	1 mL
Olive oil	2 tsp.	10 mL
Grated Parmesan cheese	¼ cup	60 mL
Dried mixed Italian herbs	1 tsp.	5 mL
Pepper, sprinkle		
All-purpose flour	2 cups	500 mL

SAUCE

Small onion, cut into 4 pieces	1	1
Garlic cloves, halved	3	3
Olive oil	1 tbsp.	15 mL
Can of stewed tomatoes, with liquid	14 oz.	398 mL
Can of plum tomatoes, with liquid	14 oz.	398 mL
Dried sweet basil	1 tsp.	5 mL
Dried marjoram	½ tsp.	2 mL
Granulated sugar	½ tsp.	2 mL
Water	3 qts.	3 L
Salt	1 tbsp.	15 mL

Gnocchi: Cut potato in 4 pieces. Cover. Boil in water and salt in small saucepan for about 10 minutes until soft when poked with a sharp knife. Drain. Cool. Peel off and discard skin. Secure knife blade in food processor. Place potato in processor bowl.

Add next 5 ingredients. Pulse with on/off motion 8 to 10 times until potato is mealy and no large pieces remain. Process until mixture starts to cling together and form a ball. Turn out dough onto lightly floured surface. Knead for about 1 minute. Let dough rest, covered with plastic wrap for 15 minutes. Divide dough into 4 portions. Roll each portion into a long rope, no more than ½ inch (1.2 cm) in diameter and about 30 inches (75 cm) long. Cut into ½ to 1 inch (1.2 to 2.5 cm) pieces. Repeat with remaining dough. As gnocchi are prepared, keep them on lightly floured tray, covered with a clean tea towel. Makes 1¼ lbs. (560 g).

(continued on next page)

Food Processor

Sauce: Put onion and garlic into food processor bowl. Pulse with on/off motion until minced. Cook in olive oil in large non-stick frying pan until soft and golden.

Drain juice from canned tomatoes into frying pan. Purée tomatoes in processor. Pour into frying pan. Stir in basil, marjoram and sugar. Simmer, uncovered, on medium for about 20 minutes until reduced slightly. Makes 2⅔ cups (650 mL) sauce.

Boil gnocchi in batches in water and salt in large saucepan for about 5 minutes until they float to water surface. Remove with large slotted spoon to drain. Toss with sauce. Serves 4.

1 serving: 414 Calories; 8.9 g Total Fat; 700 mg Sodium; 13 g Protein; 72 g Carbohydrate; 5 g Dietary Fiber

Pictured on page 53.

Wheat Pastry

Good whole wheat flavor to this flaky crisp pastry.

Whole wheat flour	2½ cups	625 mL
Cold lard, cut up	¾ cup	175 mL
Brown sugar, packed	1 tbsp.	15 mL
Baking powder	½ tsp.	2 mL
Salt	½ tsp.	2 mL
Cold water	⅓ cup	75 mL

Secure knife blade in food processor. Add flour, lard, brown sugar, baking powder and salt. Cover.

Pulse with on/off motion 4 times. Add water through feed chute. Process for about 10 seconds until dough forms a ball. Makes three 9 inch (22 cm) single pie shells or 3 casserole topping crusts.

⅓ pastry: 867 Calories; 56.4 g Total Fat; 462 mg Sodium; 14 g Protein; 81 g Carbohydrate; 13 g Dietary Fiber

Variation: Vegetable shortening can be used in place of lard.

Pie Pastry

My favorite pastry made easier in a food processor.

All-purpose flour	2½ cups	625 mL
Brown sugar, packed	1 tbsp.	15 mL
Baking powder	½ tsp.	2 mL
Salt	½ tsp.	2 mL
Cold lard (1 cup, 250 mL), cut up	½ lb.	225 g
Egg yolk (large)	1	1
White vinegar	1 tbsp.	15 mL
Cold water		

Secure knife blade in food processor. Add flour, brown sugar, baking powder, salt and lard. Cover. Pulse with on/off motion 12 to 15 times until lard is in pea-sized chunks.

Beat egg yolk with fork in measuring cup. Add vinegar. Pour in water to make total of ½ cup (125 mL). With machine running, slowly pour water mixture through feed chute. Process until dough forms a ball. Shape dough into 3 portions. Wrap in plastic and chill for up to 2 weeks or freeze for up to 2 months. Makes three 9 inch (22 cm) single pie shells or 1 double crust pie and 1 single pie shell.

1 single pie shell: 1116 Calories; 77.8 g Total Fat; 461 mg Sodium; 12 g Protein; 89 g Carbohydrate; 3 g Dietary Fiber

Variation: Vegetable shortening can be used in place of lard.

Shortbread

A special cookie for a special occasion. Whip up dough in food processor and bake in toaster oven or regular oven.

All-purpose flour	1¾ cups	425 mL
Cornstarch	¼ cup	60 mL
Icing (confectioner's) sugar	⅓ cup	75 mL
Vanilla	½ tsp.	2 mL
Salt, just a pinch		
Butter (not margarine), softened slightly and cut up	1 cup	250 mL

(continued on next page)

Secure knife disc in food processor. Measure all 6 ingredients into food processor bowl. Cover. Process for about 10 seconds until dough forms a ball. Shape into 2 rolls about 1¼ inches (3 cm) in diameter. Roll in waxed paper. Chill for at least 1 hour or overnight. Cut into ¼ inch (6 mm) slices. Arrange on ungreased toaster pan. Bake in 325°F (160°C) toaster oven for 12 to 15 minutes or use large ungreased baking sheet and bake in regular oven. Bake in 2 or 3 batches. Makes 48.

1 shortbread: 59 Calories; 4.1 g Total Fat; 41 mg Sodium; 1 g Protein; 5 g Carbohydrate; trace Dietary Fiber

Pictured on page 54.

Variation #1: Melt 1 cup (250 mL) semisweet chocolate chips in heavy saucepan over low, stirring often, until melted. Dip ½ of each cookie into chocolate. Lay on wire rack to set.

Pictured on page 54.

Variation #2: Set about 6 semi-sweet chocolate chips on each hot cookie. Allow a few minutes to melt. Spread with tip of knife.

White Cake

Can be used for an iced cake or for strawberry shortcake.

All-purpose flour	2 cups	500 mL
Baking powder	2 tsp.	10 mL
Granulated sugar	¾ cup	175 mL
Hard margarine (or butter), softened	¼ cup	60 mL
Large eggs	2	2
Salt	¼ tsp.	1 mL
Vanilla	1 tsp.	5 mL
Milk	½ cup	125 mL

Chocolate Icing, page 77

Secure knife blade in food processor. Put first 8 ingredients into processor bowl. Process until smooth. Turn into greased 9 x 9 inch (22 x 22 cm) pan. Bake in 350°F (175°C) oven for about 30 minutes until wooden pick inserted in center comes out clean. Cool.

Spread Chocolate Icing over cake. Cuts into 16 pieces.

1 piece (with icing): 140 Calories; 4 g Total Fat; 93 mg Sodium; 3 g Protein; 23 g Carbohydrate; 1 g Dietary Fiber

Pictured on page 54.

Baby Food

Using the blender to purée fruits and vegetables is fast, easy and economical. If using one of the purée recipes for your baby's meals, you will know exactly what ingredients your little one will be eating. Adjust the taste as you like and use fresh vegetables from the garden or market. Some of these purées can also be used in soups to provide condensed nutrition and added color and flavor.

Puréed Chicken Dinner

Very economical using inexpensive fryers.

Young broiler/fryer chicken, cut into 4 pieces	3 lbs.	1.4 kg
Water	6 cups	1.5 L
Celery ribs, cut into 1 inch (2.5 cm) pieces	2	2
Small onion, sliced	1	1
Large carrots, peeled and cut into 1 inch (2.5 cm) pieces	3	3
Parsley sprigs (or 2 tsp., 10 mL, flakes)	2	2
Bay leaf	1	1
Medium potatoes, cut into chunks	2	2

Remove skin from chicken pieces and discard. Bring chicken and water to a boil in large saucepan or Dutch oven. Skim off and discard foam with spoon or small sieve.

Add next 5 ingredients. Cover. Simmer, stirring once or twice, for 1 hour.

Add potatoes. Cook for about 30 minutes until chicken is well done and vegetables are soft. Remove and discard bay leaf. Pour through strainer, reserving liquid. When cool enough to handle, remove chicken from bones. Secure knife blade in food processor. Place ½ of chicken and ½ of cooked vegetables in processor bowl. Process with about ¾ cup (175 mL) broth until puréed smooth. Repeat with remaining chicken and vegetables and another ¾ cup (175 mL) broth. Discard any remaining broth or save to make soup. Depending on age of baby, spoon into small ½ cup (125 mL) or 1 cup (250 mL) freezer containers. Seal and freeze for up to 10 weeks. Makes 5½ cups (1.4 L).

½ cup (125 mL): 110 Calories; 2 g Total Fat; 63 mg Sodium; 14 g Protein; 9 g Carbohydrate; 1 g Dietary Fiber

 tip   *If you don't have enough small containers, line muffin tin cups with plastic wrap. Fill. Cover and freeze until solid. Remove to freezer bags to store.*

Food Processor

Sweet Potato Purée

Babies love the sweet flavor and smooth texture.

Medium sweet potatoes (about 1½ lbs., 680 g),peeled and cut into 1 inch (2.5 cm) chunks	2	2
Boiling water	2 cups	500 mL

Add potato to boiling water in medium saucepan. Stir. Reduce heat to medium-low. Cover. Simmer for about 30 minutes until very tender. Drain, reserving cooking water. Cool for about 10 minutes. Secure knife blade in food processor. Purée sweet potatoes and about ½ cup (125 mL) of cooking water in processor by pulsing with on/off motion several times and then processing for 1 to 2 minutes. Use more water, 1 tsp. (5 mL) at a time, if necessary until desired consistency. Makes about 2½ cups (625 mL). Fill ice cube trays. Freeze. Turn out cubes into freezer bags. Remove as needed. Will keep for up to 6 months. Makes about 2 dozen cubes.

1 cube: 21 Calories; 0.1 g Total Fat; 3 mg Sodium; trace Protein; 5 g Carbohydrate; 1 g Dietary Fiber

Puréed Carrots

Your baby will love the deep color and sweet taste.

Medium carrots (about 1¼ lbs., 560 g), peeled and cut into 1 inch (2.5 cm) pieces	6	6
Boiling water	1½ cups	375 mL

Add carrots to boiling water in medium saucepan. Reduce heat to medium-low. Cover. Simmer for about 30 minutes until very tender. Drain, reserving cooking water. Cool for about 10 minutes. Secure knife blade in food processor. Purée carrots and about ½ cup (125 mL) of cooking water in processor by pulsing with on/off motion several times and then processing for 1 to 2 minutes. Use more water, 1 tsp. (5 mL) at a time, if necessary until desired consistency. Makes about 2½ cups (625 mL). Fill ice cube trays. Freeze. Turn out cubes into freezer bags. Remove as needed. Will keep for up to 6 months. Makes about 2 dozen cubes.

1 cube: 9 Calories; 0 g Total Fat; 7 mg Sodium; trace Protein; 2 g Carbohydrate; trace Dietary Fiber

Squash Purée

Full of vitamin A. So easy to make.

Acorn or butternut squash (about 2 lbs., 900 g)	1	1
Water		

Bake whole squash in 350°F (175°C) oven for 1½ hours. Cut in half. Discard seeds and fibers from inside.

Secure knife blade in food processor. Scrape flesh from squash into processor bowl. Add about ⅓ cup (75 mL) water. Pulse with on/off motion several times. Purée. Use more water, 1 tsp. (5 mL) at a time, if necessary until desired consistency. Makes about 2½ cups (625 mL). Fill ice cube trays. Freeze. Turn out cubes into freezer bags. Remove as needed. Will keep for up to 6 months. Makes about 2 dozen cubes.

1 cube: 10 Calories; 0.1 g Total Fat; 1 mg Sodium; trace g Protein; 2 g Carbohydrate; trace Dietary Fiber

Broccoli Purée

Use the stems of the broccoli for your next stir-fry. Baby only loves the best part!

Broccoli florets (about 1 lb., 454 g, or two large bunches)	8 cups	2 L
Boiling water	1½ cups	375 mL

Add broccoli to boiling water in a large saucepan. Cover. Reduce heat to low. Cook for 8 to 10 minutes until tender but still bright green. Drain, reserving cooking water. Cool for about 10 minutes. Secure knife blade in food processor. Purée ½ of broccoli and about ¼ cup (60 mL) cooking water in processor by pulsing with on/off motion several times and then processing for 3 to 4 minutes. Use more water, 1 tsp. (5 mL) at a time, if necessary until desired consistency. Makes about 2½ cups (625 mL). Fill ice cube trays. Freeze. Turn out cubes into freezer bags. Remove as needed. Will keep for up to 6 months. Makes about 2 dozen cubes.

1 cube: 5 Calories; 0.1 g Total Fat; 5 mg Sodium; 1 g Protein; 1 g Carbohydrate; trace Dietary Fiber

Hand Blender

The two-speed hand blender was used for testing these recipes. Read your owner's manual to learn about your model's features and limitations. Hand blenders are designed for use with soft-textured food. For best results and to protect the motor, pieces of food should be no larger than 1 inch (2.5 cm).

Berry Diet Shake

A great snack when you feel like having a treat.

Cold skim milk	1 cup	250 mL
Whole fresh strawberries (or frozen, partially thawed)	8	8
Liquid honey	1 tsp.	5 mL
Vanilla	1 tsp.	5 mL

Pour milk into beaker or tall, slim container. Process with hand blender on high speed until frothy.

Add strawberries, honey and vanilla. Process on high until smooth. Serve immediately. Makes 2⅓ cups (575 mL).

1 cup (250 mL): 70 Calories; 0.4 g Total Fat; 58 mg Sodium; 4 g Protein; 12 g Carbohydrate; 1 g Dietary Fiber

Basil Pesto

Very easy to pop a cube or two into your next batch of pasta sauce or soup, or try thawed and spread on pizza, baguette slices for bruschetta.

Garlic cloves, quartered	3	3
Pine nuts, toasted	3 tbsp.	50 mL
Olive oil	⅓ cup	75 mL
Salt	½ tsp.	2 mL
Pepper	⅛ tsp.	0.5 mL
Olive oil	⅓ cup	75 mL
Packed fresh sweet basil leaves	1 cup	250 mL
Packed fresh parsley, stems removed	½ cup	125 mL
Grated Parmesan (or Romano) cheese	⅓ cup	75 mL

Place garlic, pine nuts, first amount of olive oil, salt and pepper in beaker or small deep bowl. Process with hand blender on high speed until garlic and nuts are broken up.

Add second amount of olive oil, basil and parsley. Process with hand blender on High, pulsing on and off frequently until pesto is almost smooth. Stir in Parmesan cheese. Makes about 1 cup (250 mL). Fill ice cube tray with about 1½ tbsp. (25 mL) in each section. Freeze. Turn out cubes into freezer bags. Remove as needed. Will keep for up to 6 months. Makes 1 dozen cubes.

1 cube: 142 Calories; 14.9 g Total Fat; 169 mg Sodium; 2 g Protein; 1 g Carbohydrate; 1 g Dietary Fiber

Pictured on page 71.

Freezing fresh basil is a good way to store it for future use. Place chopped basil in an ice cube tray. Cover with water. Freeze. Remove cubes to a resealable freezer bag. To use, drop a cube into soup, sauce or stew.

Hand Blender

Red Pepper Dip

Surround with vegetables or crackers. You'll also want to try this on grilled fish. Delicious!

Can of red peppers, drained and chopped	14 oz.	398 mL
Light sour cream	½ cup	125 mL
Light mayonnaise (not salad dressing)	½ cup	125 mL
Lemon juice	1 tsp.	5 mL
No-salt Italian herb mix (such as Mrs. Dash)	1½ tbsp.	25 mL
Garlic powder	¼ tsp.	1 mL

Put all 6 ingredients into deep medium bowl. Process with hand blender on high speed until smooth. Chill for at least 1 hour to allow flavors to blend. Makes about 2 cups (500 mL).

2 tbsp. (30 mL): 36 Calories; 2.7 g Total Fat; 80 mg Sodium; trace Protein; 3 g Carbohydrate; trace Dietary Fiber

Pictured on page 71.

Shrimp Spread

Makes exquisite canapés. Looks great on dark, tiny bread or bagel slices, or small crackers.

Fresh cooked shrimp (or canned)	4 oz.	113 g
Hard margarine (or butter), softened	¼ cup	60 mL
Chopped onion	2 tbsp.	30 mL
Chili sauce	2 tsp.	10 mL
Lemon juice	1 tsp.	5 mL
Light salad dressing (or mayonnaise)	¼ cup	60 mL
Cayenne pepper	¹⁄₁₆ tsp.	0.5 mL

Put all 7 ingredients into deep small bowl. Process with hand blender on high speed until a few tiny pieces remain or until smooth if you prefer. Chill. Makes 1 cup (250 mL).

2 tbsp. (30 mL): 91 Calories; 8 g Total Fat; 176 mg Sodium; 3 g Protein; 2 g Carbohydrate; trace Dietary Fiber

Pictured on page 69.

Spicy Peanut Sauce

This smooth, thick sauce "bites back" at you!

Chopped onion	½ cup	125 mL
Garlic clove, minced	1	1
Cooking oil	2 tsp.	10 mL
Smooth peanut butter	½ cup	125 mL
Water	2 tbsp.	30 mL
Chili sauce	1 tbsp.	15 mL
Lemon juice	1 tbsp.	15 mL
Corn syrup	1 tbsp.	15 mL
Soy sauce	2 tsp.	10 mL
Cayenne pepper	¼ tsp.	1 mL

Sauté onions and garlic in cooking oil in small frying pan until soft and clear. Transfer to beaker or deep small bowl.

Add remaining 7 ingredients. Process with hand blender on high speed until smooth. Makes 1 cup (250 mL).

1 tbsp. (15 mL): 60 Calories; 4.6 g Total Fat; 95 mg Sodium; 2 g Protein; 4 g Carbohydrate; 1 g Dietary Fiber

1. Basil Pesto, page 68 (tossed with linguine) **(Hand Blender)**
2. Red Pepper Dip, page 69 **(Hand Blender)**
3. Shrimp Spread, page 69 **(Hand Blender)**
4. Black Bean Soup, page 74 **(Hand Blender)**

Props Courtesy Of: Hamilton Beach
Le Gnome
Winners Stores

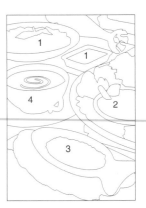

Hand Blender

Herbed Feta Dip

So good with fresh vegetables or torn pita bread.

Dried tomato slices, quartered	4	4
Boiling water	⅓ cup	75 mL
Olive oil	1 tbsp.	15 mL
Feta cheese	4 oz	113 g
Light cream cheese	4 oz.	125 g
Granulated sugar	¾ tsp.	4 mL
Dried whole oregano	½ tsp.	2 mL
Dried sweet basil	½ tsp.	2 mL
Freshly ground pepper, sprinkle		
Chopped ripe olives, drained (optional)	1 tbsp.	15 mL

Combine tomato, boiling water and olive oil in beaker or deep small bowl. Let stand for 5 minutes.

Add next 7 ingredients. Process with hand blender on high speed until creamy. Chill for at least 1 hour to allow flavors to blend. Makes 1¼ cups (300 mL).

2 tbsp. (30 mL): 69 Calories; 5.8 g Total Fat; 240 mg Sodium; 3 g Protein; 2 g Carbohydrate; trace Dietary Fiber

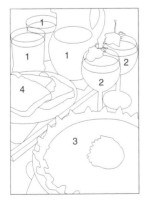

1. Berry Drink Concentrate, page 83 **(Juicer)**
2. Melon Drink, page 81 **(Juicer)**
3. Date Pie, page 78 **(Hand Blender)**
4. Tropical Loaf, page 91 **(Juicer)**

Props Courtesy Of: The Bay

Garden Pea Soup

Fresh green color with quite a different flavor from split pea soup.

Medium onion, chopped	1	1
Margarine (or butter)	2 tsp.	10 mL
Ground marjoram	½ tsp.	2 mL
Ground thyme	½ tsp.	2 mL
Small bay leaf	1	1
Cans of condensed chicken broth (10 oz., 284 mL, each)	2	2
Water	4 cups	1 L
Cubed potato (about 1 lb., 454 g)	2 cups	500 mL
Fresh (or frozen) peas	4 cups	1 L
Salt	¼ tsp.	1 mL
Pepper	¼ tsp.	1 mL

Chopped chives, for garnish

Sauté onion in margarine in large saucepan until soft.

Add next 6 ingredients. Cover. Cook for 30 to 35 minutes until potatoes are tender. Discard bay leaf.

Add peas, salt and pepper. Cook for about 3 minutes. Blend with hand blender on high speed until smooth.

Serve with a sprinkle of chives. Makes 9⅓ cups (2.3 L).

1 cup (250 mL): 110 Calories; 1.8 g Total Fat; 563 mg Sodium; 7 g Protein; 17 g Carbohydrate; 4 g Dietary Fiber

Black Bean Soup

Dark in appearance. Excellent in flavor.

Water	8 cups	2 L
Dried black beans	2 cups	500 mL
Large green pepper, chopped	1	1
Large onion, chopped	1	1
Dried whole oregano	1 tsp.	5 mL
Chicken bouillon powder	3 tbsp.	50 mL
Garlic powder	¼ tsp.	1 mL
Seasoned salt	½ tsp.	2 mL
Pepper	¼ tsp.	1 mL

(continued on next page)

Hand Blender

Can of ham flakes, drained and broken up (or 1 cup, 250 mL, diced cooked ham)	6½ oz.	184 g
Liquid smoke	⅛ tsp.	0.5 mL
White vinegar	2 tbsp.	30 mL
Sour cream, for garnish	3 tbsp.	50 mL

Combine first 9 ingredients in large pot or Dutch oven. Cover. Cook slowly for about 1½ hours until beans are soft. Purée with hand blender to desired consistency.

Add ham, liquid smoke and vinegar. Stir. Heat through.

Garnish individual servings with a swirl of sour cream. Makes 9½ cups (2.4 L).

1 cup (250 mL): 212 Calories; 4.8 g Total Fat; 955 mg Sodium; 13 g Protein; 30 g Carbohydrate; trace Dietary Fiber

Pictured on page 71.

Split Pea Soup

Definitely a favorite. Lots of flavor in this smooth soup.

Water	8 cups	2 L
Dried green split peas	1 cup	250 mL
Chopped onion	¾ cup	175 mL
Medium carrots, cut up	2	2
Bay leaf	1	1
Dried sweet basil	¼ tsp.	1 mL
Salt	½ tsp.	2 mL
Pepper	¼ tsp.	1 mL
Diced ham (or 2 cans ham flakes, 6½ oz., 184 g, each, drained)	2 cups	500 mL

Light sour cream (or plain yogurt), for garnish

Measure first 9 ingredients into large pot or Dutch oven. Bring to a boil. Cover. Simmer for about 2 hours, stirring occasionally, until split peas are tender. Discard bay leaf. Process with hand blender on high speed until smooth.

Serve with a swirl of sour cream. Makes 9 cups (2.25 L).

1 cup (250 mL): 136 Calories; 1.8 g Total Fat; 588 mg Sodium; 13 g Protein; 18 g Carbohydrate; 4 g Dietary Fiber

Chocolate Cake

Nice moist cake. Good choice.

All-purpose flour	1⅓ cups	325 mL
Granulated sugar	1 cup	250 mL
Baking soda	1 tsp.	5 mL
Salt	½ tsp.	2 mL
Cocoa, sifted if lumpy	¼ cup	60 mL
Hard margarine (or butter), melted	¼ cup	60 mL
Large eggs	2	2
Sour milk (1½ tsp., 7 mL, white vinegar plus milk)	½ cup	125 mL
Boiling water	½ cup	125 mL
Vanilla	1 tsp.	5 mL

Chocolate Icing, page 77

Measure first 10 ingredients into deep large bowl. Process with hand blender on high speed until smooth. Turn into greased 9 x 9 inch (22 x 22 cm) pan. Bake in 350°F (175°C) oven for 30 to 40 minutes until wooden pick inserted in center comes out clean. Cool.

Spread Chocolate Icing over cake. Cuts into 16 pieces.

1 piece (with icing): 216 Calories; 7 g Total Fat; 252 mg Sodium; 3 g Protein; 38 g Carbohydrate; 2 g Dietary Fiber

Paré Pointer

Johnny wanted to quit school after only one day.
He couldn't read or write, and he wasn't allowed to talk,
so what was the use?

Chocolate Icing

Satisfying flavor. Use to ice White Cake, page 63, or Chocolate Cake, page 76.

Icing (confectioner's) sugar	1¾ cups	425 mL
Cocoa, sifted if lumpy	⅓ cup	75 mL
Hard margarine (or butter), softened	¼ cup	60 mL
Hot prepared coffee (or hot water)	3 tbsp.	50 mL
Vanilla	½ tsp.	2 mL

Place all 5 ingredients in deep medium bowl. Process with hand blender on high speed until smooth, adding more icing sugar or water to make proper spreading consistency. Makes 1 cup (250 mL).

1 tbsp. (15 mL): 80 Calories; 3.1 g Total Fat; 35 mg Sodium; trace Protein; 14 g Carbohydrate; 1 g Dietary Fiber

Pictured on page 54.

Butter Icing

A basic frosting that can change flavors by changing the kind of liquid used.

Icing (confectioner's) sugar	3½ cups	875 mL
Hard margarine (or butter), softened	3 tbsp.	50 mL
Milk	¼ cup	60 mL
Vanilla	1 tsp.	5 mL

Beat all 4 ingredients in deep small bowl with hand blender on high speed until smooth, adding more icing sugar or milk as needed for proper spreading consistency. Makes 1⅔ cups (400 mL).

1 tbsp. (15 mL): 72 Calories; 1.3 g Total Fat; 16 mg Sodium; trace Protein; 16 g Carbohydrate; 0 g Dietary Fiber

COFFEE ICING: Omit milk and add ¼ cup (60 mL) cooled strong coffee. Color will be deep caramel.

Date Pie

This rich pie filling fits perfectly into a commercial pie shell.
If using your own, increase the recipe by half.

Chopped dates	1 cup	250 mL
Boiling water	1 cup	250 mL
Light sour cream	1 cup	250 mL
Large egg	1	1
All-purpose flour	2 tbsp.	30 mL
Granulated sugar	½ cup	125 mL
Lemon juice	1 tsp.	5 mL
Salt	⅛ tsp.	0.5 mL
Ground cinnamon	¼ tsp.	1 mL
Ground nutmeg	⅛ tsp.	0.5 mL
Unbaked 9 inch (22 cm) pie shell	1	1
Ground nutmeg, for garnish	½ tsp.	2 mL

Combine dates and boiling water in deep medium bowl. Cover. Let stand for 15 minutes. Drain.

Add next 8 ingredients. Process with hand blender on high speed until dates are mixed in.

Pour into pie shell. Sprinkle with nutmeg. Bake in 350°F (175°C) oven for about 40 minutes until set and pastry is browned. Cuts into 8 wedges.

1 wedge: 260 Calories; 10.4 g Total Fat; 204 mg Sodium; 4 g Protein; 40 g Carbohydrate; 2 g Dietary Fiber

Pictured on page 72.

 For thorough mixing, move hand blender up and down in container until mixture is smooth.

Hand Blender

Juicer

We tested these recipes using a one-speed juicer. Read your owner's manual to learn about your model's features and limitations. Always prepare fruits and vegetables as if for eating: wash to avoid contamination and remove pits and stones. **Always push fruits and vegetables into the feed chute using the pusher that comes with your machine — do not use your fingers!** If food gets stuck, unplug cord and disassemble to dislodge. Since many juices tend to be concentrated or dense, dilute to taste with club soda or ginger-ale.

Orchard Juice

Good rich flavor.

Firm medium pears, cored	3	3
Medium apples, cored	3	3
Nectarines (or peaches), pitted	2	2
Medium plums, pitted	4	4
Apricots, pitted	3	3
Liquid honey (optional)	1-2 tbsp.	15-30 mL

Cut fruit to fit juicer feed chute. Push fruit through chute, alternating apple pieces with softer fruits. Juice will be foamy and will settle into layers. Stir well and serve immediately.

If apples and plums are quite tart you can sweeten to taste with honey. Makes 3½ cups (875 mL).

½ cup (125 mL): 77 Calories; 0.1 g Total Fat; 6 mg Sodium; trace Protein; 20 g Carbohydrate; 1 g Dietary Fiber

Very Berry Juice

Soft, ripe berries yield the most juice. Use as a topping for ice cream.

Fresh strawberries	12 oz.	340 g
Fresh blueberries	1½ cups	375 mL
Fresh raspberries	6 oz.	170 g

Push all 3 fruits through juicer feed chute. Makes 2 cups (500 mL) juice and 1½ cups (375 mL) pulp.

½ cup (125 mL) juice: 45 Calories; 0.4 g Total Fat; 2 mg Sodium; 1 g Protein; 11 g Carbohydrate; 3 g Dietary Fiber

Pictured on front cover.

Fruit Punch

Some of the pulp can be stirred back into the juice for a thicker drink.

Medium cantaloupe, peeled and seeded	½	½
Seedless red or green grapes	½ cup	125 mL
Small apple, with peel, quartered and cored	1	1
Fresh cranberries	½ cup	125 mL
Fresh medium strawberries, stems removed	6	6

Cut cantaloupe into pieces to fit juicer feed chute. Push all fruit through chute. Makes 1½ cups (375 mL) juice and 1⅓ cups (325 mL) pulp.

½ cup (125 mL) juice: 50 Calories; 0.4 g Total Fat; 4 mg Sodium; 1 g Protein; 13 g Carbohydrate; 2 g Dietary Fiber

---

Paré Pointer

The moon is like money in your pocket;
at times it gets down to its last quarter.

Orange Vegetable Brew

Subtle squash and celery flavor. Carrots and sweet potatoes add a pleasant sweetness. Serve with a celery rib "stir stick."

Medium carrots (about 1 lb., 454 g)	8	8
Medium sweet potato	1	1
Acorn (or banana) squash (about 1 lb., 454 g), peeled and seeded	1	1
Medium celery ribs	3	3

Cut vegetables into pieces to fit juicer feed chute. Push vegetables through chute, one at time. Makes 2¼ cups (550 mL).

½ cup (125 mL) juice: 42 Calories; 0.2 g Total Fat; 22 mg Sodium; 1 g Protein; 10 g Carbohydrate; 1 g Dietary Fiber

Pictured on page 89.

Melon Drink

An equal amount of pulp may be stirred into the juice if desired and eaten with a spoon.

Medium cantaloupe, peeled and seeded	½	½
Peaches (or nectarines), pitted	2	2
Medium apple, with peel, cored	1	1
Apricots, pitted	3	3
Green grapes, cantaloupe pieces, maraschino cherries, for garnish		

Cut fruit to fit juicer feed chute. Push all 4 fruits through chute.

Push 1 grape, 1 cantaloupe piece and 1 cherry on plastic sword. Set on rim of glass. Makes 2 cups (500 mL) juice and 1¾ cups (425 mL) pulp.

½ cup (125 mL) juice: 40 Calories; 0.2 g Total Fat; 3 mg Sodium; 1 g Protein; 10 g Carbohydrate; 1 g Dietary Fiber

Pictured on page 72.

Variation: Omit 1 peach. Add ½ papaya.

Tropical Breeze

Delicious tropical flavor. Serve chilled over ice with a splash of soda water if desired. Use the pulp in Tropical Loaf, page 91.

Papaya, peeled and seeded	½	½
Mango, peeled and pitted	1	1
Fresh pineapple slices, peeled and cored	2	2

Cut fruit to fit juicer feed chute. Push all 3 fruits through chute. Makes 2⅓ cups (575 mL) juice and 1 cup (250 mL) pulp.

½ cup (125 mL) juice: 45 Calories; 0.3 g Total Fat; 2 mg Sodium; trace Protein; 12 g Carbohydrate; 1 g Dietary Fiber

Pictured on front cover.

Fizzy Ale

Refreshing — and for what "ails" you! Serve chilled over ice.

Green seedless grapes	1½ lbs.	680 g
Large lemon, with peel, cut into 6 wedges (see Note)	1 wedge	1 wedge
Slice of gingerroot (about 1½ inches, 3.8 cm, in diameter)	¼ inch	6 mm
Sparkling mineral water	2 cups	500 mL

Push grapes through juicer feed chute. Remove thin layer of yellow peel from lemon, leaving white pith on the fruit. Push through chute. Push gingerroot slice through chute. Discard all pulp.

Stir in mineral water. Makes 3¾ cups (925 mL).

½ cup (125 mL) undiluted: 78 Calories; 0.1 g Total Fat; 4 mg Sodium; 1 g Protein; 19 g Carbohydrate; trace Dietary Fiber

Note: Store remaining 5 wedges in refrigerator or freezer for future use.

Berry Drink Concentrate

Can also be mixed with sparkling water or soda.

Fresh raspberries	3½ cups	875 mL
Fresh blueberries	2 cups	500 mL
Large lemon, with peel, cut into 6 wedges (see Note)	2 wedges	2 wedges
Granulated sugar	4 tsp.	20 mL
Lemon-lime soft drink	4½ cups	1.1 L

Push fruit through juicer feed chute. Stir in sugar until dissolved. Makes ¾ cup (175 mL), enough for 6 servings.

For 1 serving, stir 2 tbsp. (30 mL) concentrate into ¾ cup (175 mL) soft drink. Serve over ice.

¾ cup (175 mL) with soft drink: 87 Calories; 0.1 g Total Fat; 19 mg Sodium; trace Protein; 23 g Carbohydrate; 1 g Dietary Fiber

Pictured on page 72.

Note: Store remaining 4 wedges in refrigerator or freezer for future use.

Straw-Barb Juice

Pretty pink color. Slightly tart flavor is so good mixed with ginger ale.

Fresh strawberries, stems removed	6 oz.	170 g
Fresh rhubarb ribs, cut into pieces	2	2
Liquid honey	2 tbsp.	30 mL
Ginger ale soft drink (see Note)	1 cup	250 mL

Push fruit through juicer feed chute, 1 piece at a time. Add honey. Stir well. Pour in ginger ale. Makes 2 cups (500 mL).

½ cup (125 mL): 79 Calories; 0.3 g Total Fat; 8 mg Sodium; 1 g Protein; 20 g Carbohydrate; 2 g Dietary Fiber

Note: Other soft drink flavors, such as cream soda, lemon-lime, or soda water, can be used.

Beet Bonanza

So good and so good for you!

Medium beets	2	2
Medium carrots	6	6
Medium English cucumber	1	1
Medium celery ribs	2	2
Small apple	1	1

Scrub vegetables. Do not peel. Cut into chunks to fit juicer feed chute. Push chunks, 1 at a time, through chute. Makes 2¼ cups (550 mL).

½ cup (125 mL): 34 Calories; 0.1 g Total Fat; 29 mg Sodium; 1 g Protein; 8 g Carbohydrate; 1 Dietary Fiber

Pictured on page 89.

Green Zinger

An easy way to "eat" enough green vegetables.

Medium zucchini, with peel	1	1
Medium English cucumber, with peel	1	1
Small apple, with peel, cored	1	1
Green beans	1 cup	250 mL
Pea pods	1 cup	250 mL
Large dark green lettuce leaves	4	4
Fresh parsley sprigs	3	3
Spinach leaves	15	15

Cut zucchini, cucumber and apple to fit juicer feed chute. Push through chute. Push beans and pea pods through chute.

Roll lettuce leaves tightly with parsley. Push through chute.

Stack 5 spinach leaves and roll tightly. Push through chute. Repeat twice. Makes 1⅔ cups (400 mL).

½ cup (125 mL): 16 Calories; 0.1 g Total Fat; 5 mg Sodium; 1 g Protein; 4 g Carbohydrate; 1 g Dietary Fiber

Pictured on page 89.

Winter Veggies Drink

Not getting enough orange veggies? This is the answer.

Small turnip, peeled	1	1
Medium carrots	4	4
Small parsnips	6	6

Carrot coin "flower", for garnish

Taste a small sliver of turnip first. If it is very strong in flavor, use a little less and increase carrots and parsnips. Cut turnip to fit juicer feed chute. Push all 3 vegetables through chute.

Garnish glasses with carrot flower. Makes 1⅔ cups (400 mL).

½ cup (125 mL): 41 Calories; 0.2 g Total Fat; 32 mg Sodium; 1 g Protein; 10 g Carbohydrate; 2 g Dietary Fiber

Pictured on page 89.

Spicy Veggie Brew

If you don't have a small hot pepper, shake in some hot pepper sauce to spice it up just the way you like it!

Large orange or red pepper	1	1
Broccoli florets (about ½ head)	8 oz.	225 g
Medium carrots	2	2
Medium celery ribs	2	2
Medium English cucumber, with peel	½	½
Small hot pepper, seeded (see Tip, page 49)	1	1
Medium roma (plum) tomatoes	4	4

Cut vegetables into pieces to fit juicer feed chute. Push through chute, 1 at a time. Makes 2 cups (500 mL).

½ cup (125 mL): 26 Calories; 0.2 g Total Fat; 78 mg Sodium; 1 g Protein; 6 g Carbohydrate; 1 g Dietary Fiber

Vegetable Pulp Soup

Makes a big batch of mellow-flavored soup in only 30 minutes.
A delicious way to use leftover pulp from juicer.

Chopped onion	1 cup	250 mL
Garlic, minced	1	1
Cooking oil	1 tbsp.	15 mL
Vegetable pulp (from Orange Vegetable Brew, page 81)	4 cups	1 L
Cans of condensed chicken broth (10 oz., 284 mL, each)	2	2
Water	6 cups	1.5 L
Salt	½ tsp.	2 mL
Pepper	¼ tsp.	1 mL
Potatoes, peeled and diced	1½ cups	375 mL
Turnip, peeled and diced	1⅔ cups	400 mL
Bay leaf	1	1
Chicken bouillon powder	1 tbsp.	15 mL
Ground thyme	¼ tsp.	1 mL
Ground savory	¼ tsp.	1 mL

Sauté onion and garlic in cooking oil in Dutch oven until soft.

Add next 11 ingredients. Bring to a boil. Reduce heat. Simmer for 30 minutes until potatoes and turnips are tender. Discard bay leaf. Makes 10¾ cups (2.7 L) soup.

1 cup (250 mL): 85 Calories; 2.2 g Total Fat; 688 mg Sodium; 4 g Protein; 13 g Carbohydrate; 2 g Dietary Fiber

 To get clear juice from juicer, strain through a coffee filter or several layers of cheesecloth.

Carrot Cake

Lots of good "stuff" in this cake. Uses juicer instead of grater to prepare carrots.

Granulated sugar	1 cup	250 mL
Large eggs	3	3
Cooking oil	¾ cup	175 mL
Vanilla	1½ tsp.	7 mL
Carrot pulp (see Note)	1½ cups	375 mL
Carrot juice (see Note)	½ cup	125 mL
Can of crushed pineapple, with juice	8 oz.	227 mL
Chopped walnuts (optional)	1 cup	250 mL
All-purpose flour	2 cups	500 mL
Baking powder	1½ tsp.	7 mL
Baking soda	1½ tsp.	7 ml
Salt	¾ tsp.	4 mL
Ground cinnamon	1½ tsp.	7 mL

CREAM CHEESE ICING

Light cream cheese, softened	8 oz.	250 g
Hard margarine, softened	¼ cup	60 g
Icing (confectioner's) sugar	2½ cups	625 mL
Vanilla	1½ tsp.	7 mL

Beat sugar and eggs in large bowl. Add cooking oil, vanilla, carrot pulp and carrot juice. Beat. Add pineapple with juice and walnuts. Stir.

Add flour, baking powder, baking soda, salt and cinnamon. Stir until moistened. Turn into greased 9 x 13 inch (22 x 33 cm) baking pan. Bake in 350°F (175°C) oven for 45 to 50 minutes until wooden pick inserted in center comes out clean.

Cream Cheese Icing: Beat cream cheese, margarine and about ½ of icing sugar well in medium bowl. Gradually beat in remaining icing sugar and vanilla. Makes 2 cups (500 mL) icing. Ice cooled cake. Cuts into 20 pieces.

1 piece (with icing): 300 Calories; 14.1 g Total Fat; 369 mg Sodium; 4 g Protein; 40 g Carbohydrate; 1 g Dietary Fiber

Note: Nine medium carrots pushed through juicer will yield about 1½ cups (375 mL) pulp and about 1 cup (250 mL) juice. Drink the remaining ½ cup (125 mL) juice or save for future use.

Very Berry Syrup

Deep burgundy in color. Use on pancakes, waffles, crêpes and ice cream.

Berry pulp (from Very Berry Juice, page 80), pressed through sieve to remove seeds	1 cup	250 mL
Granulated sugar	1 cup	250 mL
Water	1 cup	250 mL
Lemon juice	1 tsp.	5 mL

Stir all 4 ingredients in medium saucepan until sugar is dissolved. Bring to a boil. Reduce heat. Simmer for 15 minutes to reduce and thicken. Makes 1⅔ cups (400 mL) syrup.

2 tbsp. (30 mL): 68 Calories; 0.1 g Total Fat; 1 mg Sodium; trace Protein; 17 g Carbohydrate; 1 g Dietary Fiber

Pictured on page 17.

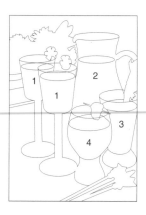

1. Winter Veggies Drink, page 85 (Juicer)
2. Green Zinger, page 85 (Juicer)
3. Orange Vegetable Brew, page 81 (Juicer)
4. Beet Bonanza, page 84 (Juicer)

Props Courtesy Of: Hamilton Beach
Stokes

Tropical Loaf

Makes a small loaf with exceptional flavor using leftover fruit pulp from juicer. Because of the pulp, this loaf may not peak.

Hard margarine (or butter), softened	½ cup	125 mL
Granulated sugar	1 cup	250 mL
Large eggs	2	2
Fruit pulp (from Tropical Breeze, page 82)	1 cup	250 mL
All-purpose flour	2 cups	500 mL
Baking soda	1 tsp.	5 mL
Baking powder	½ tsp.	2 mL
Salt	½ tsp.	2 mL
Coconut (or chopped nuts), optional	¼ cup	60 mL

Cream margarine and sugar together in medium bowl. Add eggs, 1 at a time, beating until smooth. Blend in fruit pulp.

Stir flour, baking soda, baking powder and salt together in small bowl. Add to fruit mixture and stir until just moistened. Gently stir in coconut. Turn into greased 8 x 4 x 3 inch (20 x 10 x 7.5 cm) loaf pan. Bake at 350°F (175°C) for 65 minutes until wooden pick inserted in center comes out clean. Makes 1 loaf. Cuts into 16 slices.

1 slice: 182 Calories; 6.9 g Total Fat; 251 mg Sodium; 3 g Protein; 28 g Carbohydrate; 1 g Dietary Fiber

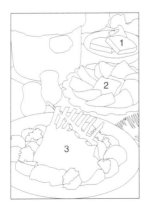

1. Chocolate Pudding Cake, page 109
   (Pressure Cooker)
2. White Fruitcake, page 112
   (Pressure Cooker)
3. Rack Of Lamb, page 101
   (Pressure Cooker)

Props Courtesy Of: Le Gnome
                    Zenari's

Pressure Cooker

Under steam pressure, food inside a pressure cooker cooks faster than in a regular saucepan or Dutch oven. The 6 quart (6 L) pressure cooker used for testing these recipes showed 15 lbs. (6.8 kg) of pressure when pressure regulator rocked. Read your owner's manual to learn your model's features and limitations. Pressure cooking requires liquid to steam food in or the food will scorch. Always check to see if the hole in the lid is clear so excess steam can escape. Don't fill pressure cooker more than ⅔ full in order to allow for even cooking. **Don't open a pressure cooker when it's under pressure — contents may explode and cause harm!**

French Onion Soup

*Good traditional flavor. Even good without broiling
if you don't have oven-proof bowls.*

Large onions, thinly sliced	4	4
Cans of condensed beef broth (10 oz., 284 mL, each)	2	2
Water	3¼ cups	800 mL
Beef bouillon powder (or liquid)	1 tbsp.	15 mL
Dry red wine (optional)	½ cup	125 mL
Unbuttered toast circles (3 inches, 7.5 cm, in diameter)	8	8
Grated part-skim mozzarella cheese	⅔ cup	150 mL

Combine first 4 ingredients in pressure cooker. Secure lid. Bring up to pressure on high heat. Reduce heat to medium. Cook for 5 minutes. Remove from heat. Let pressure drop on its own. Remove lid.

Add red wine. Ladle soup into oven-proof bowls.

Float toast circle on each soup. Divide cheese over top. Broil until cheese is melted and lightly browned. Makes 8 cups (2 L).

1 cup (250 mL): 147 Calories; 2.9 g Total Fat; 874 mg Sodium; 8 g Protein; 23 g Carbohydrate; 2 g Dietary Fiber

Seafood Chowder

This is an exceptionally good chowder. A must-try.

Bacon slices, diced	3	3
Medium onion, chopped	1	1
Grated potato	2 cups	500 mL
Medium carrot, grated	1	1
Finely chopped celery	¼ cup	60 mL
Chicken bouillon powder	2 tsp.	10 mL
Cod fillet, cubed	10 oz.	284 mL
Water	3½ cups	875 mL
Skim evaporated milk	1 cup	250 mL
All-purpose flour	¼ cup	60 mL
Salt	1 tsp.	5 mL
Pepper	⅛ tsp.	0.5 mL
Chopped cooked shrimp	1 cup	250 mL

Sauté bacon and onion in pressure cooker until golden.

Add next 6 ingredients. Secure lid. Bring up to pressure on high heat. Reduce heat to medium. Cook for 3 minutes. Remove from heat. Let pressure come down on its own. Remove lid. Heat until gently boiling.

Gradually whisk milk into flour, salt and pepper in small bowl until smooth. Stir into boiling soup until thickened.

Add shrimp. Heat through. Makes 8¾ cups (2.2 L).

1 cup (250 mL): 163 Calories; 5.2 g Total Fat; 612 mg Sodium; 14 g Protein; 15 g Carbohydrate; 1 g Dietary Fiber

 Some foods will foam excessively and should not be cooked in a pressure cooker. These include applesauce, cranberries, rhubarb, cereal, dried soup mix, pasta, split peas or pearl barley.

Vegetable Beef Soup

Perfect for a rainy day. Accompany this with crusty bread from your bread machine.

Lean ground beef	1 lb.	454 g
Chopped onion	1 cup	250 mL
Diced potato (about 1 medium)	1 cup	250 mL
Sliced carrot	1 cup	250 mL
Frozen cut green beans	½ cup	125 mL
Chopped celery	½ cup	125 mL
Dried sweet basil	½ tsp.	2 mL
Can of diced tomatoes, with juice	14 oz.	398 mL
Water	4 cups	1 L
Bay leaf	1	1
Beef bouillon powder	1 tbsp.	15 mL

Scramble-fry ground beef in pressure cooker. Drain.

Add next 10 ingredients to cooker. Mix well to distribute ground beef. Cooker should not be over ½ full. Secure lid. Bring up to pressure on high heat. Reduce heat to medium. Cook for 5 minutes. Remove from heat. Let pressure drop on its own. Remove lid. Discard bay leaf. Makes 9 cups (2.25 L).

1 cup (250 mL): 118 Calories; 4.5 g Total Fat; 303 mg Sodium; 11 g Protein; 9 g Carbohydrate; 2 g Dietary Fiber

Pictured on page 107.

Navy Bean Soup

One of those comfort foods on a cold winter's night.

Dried navy beans	1 cup	250 mL
Water, to cover		
Smoked ham hock (or salt pork)	1¼ lbs.	560 g
Water	5 cups	1.25 L

(continued on next page)

Chopped onion	½ cup	125 mL
Can of condensed chicken broth	10 oz.	284 mL
Pepper	⅛ tsp.	0.5 mL

Soak beans in water overnight. Drain.

Combine beans, ham and water in pressure cooker. Secure lid. Bring up to pressure on high heat. Reduce heat to low. Cook for 30 minutes. Remove from heat. Let pressure drop on its own. Remove lid. Remove ham. Cut ham into small pieces. Return to cooker.

Add onion, chicken broth and pepper. Stir. Cover loosely without pressure. Simmer for about 15 minutes until onion is soft. Makes 6 cups (1.5 L).

1 cup (250 mL): 437 Calories; 32.6 g Total Fat; 878 mg Sodium; 12 g Protein; 24 g Carbohydrate; 3 g Dietary Fiber

Pictured on page 107.

Beef Stew

Tender beef surrounded with vegetables and juices.

Beef stew meat, cut bite size	1½ lbs.	680 g
Medium potatoes, cubed	4	4
Medium carrots, sliced into 1 inch (2.5 cm) pieces (or use ½ medium turnip, cubed)	3	3
Sliced celery	1 cup	250 mL
Large onion, cut up	1	1
Can of condensed beef consommé	10 oz.	284 mL
Tomato paste	3 tbsp.	50 mL
Liquid gravy browner	½ tsp.	2 mL
Pepper	¼ tsp.	1 mL

Combine first 5 ingredients in pressure cooker.

Mix remaining 4 ingredients in medium bowl. Add to beef mixture. Secure lid. Bring up to pressure on high heat. Reduce heat to medium. Cook for 15 minutes. Remove from heat. Let pressure drop on its own. Remove lid. Serves 6.

1 serving: 318 Calories; 9.7 g Total Fat; 393 mg Sodium; 34 g Protein; 23 g Carbohydrate; 3 g Dietary Fiber

Stewed Beef And Dumplings

Fluffy, light biscuits in a tender meat and gravy dish.

Beef stew meat, cut bite size	1½ lbs.	680 g
Large onion, chopped	1	1
Sliced fresh mushrooms	1½ cups	375 mL
Cans of tomatoes (14 oz., 398 mL, each), with juice	2	2
Water	1 cup	250 mL
Beef bouillon powder	1-1½ tsp.	5-7 mL
Ground thyme	¼ tsp.	1 mL
Granulated sugar	1½ tsp.	7 mL
Salt	1 tsp.	5 mL
Pepper	¼ tsp.	1 mL
Cornstarch	2 tbsp.	30 mL
Water	¼ cup	60 mL
DUMPLINGS		
All-purpose flour	1⅓ cups	325 mL
Baking powder	2½ tsp.	12 mL
Granulated sugar	1½ tsp.	7 mL
Salt	½ tsp.	2 mL
Cooking oil	2 tbsp.	30 mL
Milk	⅔ cup	150 mL

Layer beef in pressure cooker. Sprinkle onion and mushrooms over top. Pour tomatoes over all.

Mix next 6 ingredients in small bowl. Add to cooker. Secure lid. Bring up to pressure on high heat. Reduce heat to medium. Cook for 15 minutes. Remove from heat. Let pressure drop on its own. Remove lid.

Combine cornstarch and water in small bowl. Stir into stew. Heat until boiling and slightly thickened. Reduce to a simmer.

Dumplings: Stir all 6 ingredients in medium bowl. Drop by tablespoonfuls onto stew. Cover loosely. Cook for 15 minutes. Makes 6 cups (1.5 L) stew and 9 dumplings. Serves 6.

1 serving: 396 Calories; 13.7 g Total Fat; 1089 mg Sodium; 31 g Protein; 36 g Carbohydrate; 3 g Dietary Fiber

Sweet And Sour Chicken

An awesome sauce covers this platter of chicken.

Skinless chicken parts	3 lbs.	1.4 kg
Cooking oil	1 tbsp.	15 mL
White vinegar	⅓ cup	75 mL
Pineapple juice	½ cup	125 mL
Brown sugar, packed	¼ cup	60 mL
Light soy sauce	2 tbsp.	30 mL
Ketchup	1 tbsp.	15 mL
Ground ginger	¼ tsp.	1 mL
Cornstarch	1½ tbsp.	25 mL
Water	1½ tbsp.	25 mL

Brown chicken in batches in hot cooking oil in pressure cooker. Remove to plate. Set rack in bottom. Place chicken on rack.

Stir next 6 ingredients together in small bowl. Pour over chicken. Secure lid. Bring up to pressure on high heat. Reduce heat to medium. Cook for 6 minutes. Remove from heat. Let pressure drop on its own. Remove lid.

Transfer chicken with slotted spoon to platter. Keep warm. Skim off and discard fat from liquid. Stir cornstarch and water in small cup. Stir into liquid in pressure cooker. Cook and stir until boiling and thickened. Pour over chicken to serve. Serves 4.

1 serving: 326 Calories; 8.3 g Total Fat; 713 mg Sodium; 37 g Protein; 24 g Carbohydrate; trace Dietary Fiber

Paré Pointer

Where did the computer girl go? She went data way.

Chicken Cacciatore

You will want to cook two cups of penne or your favorite pasta to serve with this.

Boneless, skinless chicken breast halves (about 1 lb., 454 g)	4	4
Cooking oil	1 tbsp.	15 mL
Medium onion, sliced	1	1
Sliced fresh mushrooms	1 cup	250 mL
Small green pepper, chopped	1	1
Can of diced tomatoes, with juice	14 oz.	398 mL
Apple juice	½ cup	125 mL
Water	½ cup	125 mL
Dried whole oregano	½ tsp.	2 mL
Dried sweet basil	¼ tsp.	1 mL
Granulated sugar	½ tsp.	2 mL
Salt	½ tsp.	2 mL
Pepper	¼ tsp.	1 mL
Garlic powder	¼ tsp.	1 mL
Ground cumin	¼ tsp.	1 mL
Ground rosemary	⅛ tsp.	0.5 mL

Brown chicken in hot cooking oil in pressure cooker.

Add onion, mushrooms and green pepper.

Stir remaining 11 ingredients together in medium bowl. Pour into pressure cooker. Secure lid. Bring up to pressure on high heat. Reduce heat to medium. Cook for 4 minutes. Remove from heat. Let pressure drop on its own. Remove lid. Makes 2½ cups (625 mL). Serves 4.

1 serving: 214 Calories; 5.4 g Total Fat; 425 mg Sodium; 28 g Protein; 13 g Carbohydrate; 2 g Dietary Fiber

Pictured on page 107.

 A pressure cooker is usually removed from the hot burner to let pressure reduce slowly on its own. Running the pressure cooker under cool water to reduce pressure quickly and halt the cooking process is occasionally used for delicate foods such as fruits, vegetables and custards.

Pacific Chicken

A hint of sweetness and a great aroma.

Chicken thighs and drumsticks (about 2 lbs., 900 g), skin removed	8	8
Cooking oil	1 tbsp.	15 mL
Water	¼ cup	60 mL
Brown sugar, packed	½ cup	125 mL
Garlic powder	¼ tsp.	1 mL
Ground ginger	¼ tsp.	1 mL
Light soy sauce	¼ cup	60 mL
Apple juice	½ cup	125 mL
Ketchup	1 tbsp.	15 mL
Cornstarch	2 tbsp.	30 mL
Water	2 tbsp.	30 mL

Brown chicken thighs and drumsticks in hot cooking oil in pressure cooker. Remove chicken to plate. Set rack in bottom. Place chicken on rack.

Combine next 7 ingredients in small bowl. Pour over chicken. Secure lid. Bring up to pressure on high heat. Reduce heat to medium. Cook for 5 minutes. Remove from heat. Let pressure drop on its own. Remove lid. Remove chicken to platter. Keep warm.

Skim off and discard fat from surface of liquid. Stir cornstarch and water in small cup. Stir into liquid. Heat and stir until boiling and thickened. Makes 2 cups (500 mL) sauce. Pour over chicken on platter or serve on the side. Serves 4.

1 serving: 339 Calories; 8.2 g Total Fat; 1269 mg Sodium; 27 g Protein; 39 g Carbohydrate; trace Dietary Fiber

Paré Pointer

Little kindergarten ghosts like to sing Boo Boo Black Sheep.

Lamb Curry

A delicious variation from Southern India. Serve over couscous, rice or noodles.

Boneless lamb, trimmed of fat, cubed	3 lbs.	1.4 kg
Large onion, chopped	1	1
Grated carrot	½ cup	125 mL
Boiling water	1 cup	250 mL
Beef bouillon powder	2 tsp.	10 mL
Curry powder	2 tsp.	10 mL
Ground ginger	⅛ tsp.	0.5 mL
Ground cumin	⅛ tsp.	0.5 mL
Pepper	¼ tsp.	1 mL
Medium coconut	¼ cup	60 mL
Cornstarch	2 tbsp.	30 mL
Water	2 tbsp.	30 mL
Mango chutney	½ cup	125 mL

Combine lamb, onion and carrot in pressure cooker.

Stir next 7 ingredients in small bowl. Add to lamb mixture. Secure lid. Bring up to pressure on high heat. Reduce heat to medium. Cook for 15 minutes. Remove from heat. Let pressure drop on its own. Remove lid.

Mix cornstarch and water in small cup. Stir into curry. Simmer until thickened. Stir in chutney. Makes 7 cups (1.75 L). Serves 10 to 12.

1 serving: 231 Calories; 8.9 g Total Fat; 213 mg Sodium; 28 g Protein; 8 g Carbohydrate; 1 g Dietary Fiber

Rack Of Lamb

Picturesque and flavorful. Surround with
broiled red onion wedges and fresh parsley for added color.

Water	¼ cup	60 mL
Racks of lamb (about 1⅔ lbs., 750 g, total), 7 or 8 ribs each (see Note)	2	2
Cooking oil	1 tbsp.	15 mL
Ground thyme	¼ tsp.	1 mL
Ground savory	¼ tsp.	1 mL
Ground marjoram	¼ tsp.	1 mL
Ground rosemary	¼ tsp.	1 mL
Seasoned salt	½ tsp.	2 mL
Pepper	¼ tsp.	1 mL
Parsley flakes	¼ tsp.	1 mL

Pour water into pressure cooker. Set rack in bottom.

Brush lamb with cooking oil.

Mix remaining 7 ingredients in small bowl. Coat lamb with mixture. Set lamb upright, with bones interlaced, on rack in pressure cooker. Secure lid. Bring up to pressure on high heat. Reduce heat to medium. Cook for 6 to 10 minutes until desired doneness. Remove from heat. Let pressure drop on its own. Remove lid. Serves 6.

1 serving: 361 Calories; 33.7 g Total Fat; 164 mg Sodium; 13 g Protein; trace Carbohydrate; trace Dietary Fiber

Pictured on page 90.

Note: Ask your butcher to chine or sever the backbone to make slicing between the ribs easier.

Paré Pointer

A cat has nine lives but a frog croaks all the time.

Ribs Delight

It's hard to believe ribs can be so tender in such a short time.

Prepared strong coffee	1 cup	250 mL
Chili sauce	¼ cup	60 mL
Granulated sugar	¼ cup	60 mL
Balsamic vinegar	3 tbsp.	50 mL
Steak sauce (such as HP sauce)	1½ tbsp.	25 mL
Onion powder	¼ tsp.	1 mL
Salt	¼ tsp.	1 mL
Pepper	⅛ tsp.	0.5 mL
Pork spareribs, cut into 3-rib pieces	3½ lbs.	1.6 kg

Measure first 8 ingredients into pressure cooker. Stir together well.

Add spareribs. Stir to coat. Secure lid. Bring up to pressure on high heat. Reduce heat to medium. Cook for 15 minutes. Remove from heat. Let pressure drop on its own. Remove lid. Serves 6.

1 serving: 367 Calories; 23.8 g Total Fat; 364 mg Sodium; 24 g Protein; 13 g Carbohydrate; 1 g Dietary Fiber

Pictured on front cover.

Variation: If desired, skim fat from liquid. Thicken liquid with 2 tbsp. (30 mL) cornstarch dissolved in 3 tbsp. (50 mL) water. Boil, stirring constantly, until thickened and clear. Makes about 2 cups (500 mL).

Pork Chops Supreme

The flavor is good and meat tender.
Serve with your favorite sauce, applesauce or gravy.

Water	¾ cup	175 mL
Soy sauce	⅓ cup	75 mL
Lemon pepper seasoning	2 tsp.	10 mL
Garlic powder (or 2 cloves, minced)	½ tsp.	2 mL
Parsley flakes	½ tsp.	2 mL
Bone-in pork loin chops (about 2¼ lbs., 1 kg), trimmed of fat	6	6

(continued on next page)

Pressure Cooker

Measure first 5 ingredients into pressure cooker. Stir.

Add pork chops. Secure lid. Bring up to pressure on high heat. Reduce heat to medium. Cook for 5 minutes. Remove from heat. Let pressure drop on its own. Remove lid. Serves 6.

1 serving: 166 Calories; 6.1 g Total Fat; 1029 mg Sodium; 25 g Protein; 2 g Carbohydrate; trace Dietary Fiber

Apple Pork Chops

Apple complements the pork without being sweet.

Apple juice	1 cup	250 mL
Beef bouillon powder	2 tsp.	10 mL
Dried sweet basil	¼ tsp.	1 mL
Garlic powder	¼ tsp.	1 mL
Salt	¼ tsp.	1 mL
Pepper	⅛ tsp.	0.5 mL
Pork chops (about 1¾ lbs., 790 g), trimmed of fat	4	4
Red apples, with peel, diced	2	2

Measure first 6 ingredients into pressure cooker. Stir.

Add pork chops. Scatter apple over top. Secure lid. Bring up to pressure on high heat. Reduce heat to medium. Cook for 6 to 7 minutes. Remove from heat. Let pressure drop on its own. Remove lid. Serves 4.

1 serving: 247 Calories; 7.2 g Total Fat; 542 mg Sodium; 26 g Protein; 19 g Carbohydrate; 1 g Dietary Fiber

 Reduce the cooking time of your favorite recipes by two–thirds using a pressure cooker. For example, if a roast needs 60 minutes in the oven, it needs only 20 minutes in a pressure cooker.

Pork Jambalaya

No need to go to Louisiana for a taste of Cajun cooking.

Hot sausage links (such as Chorizo or hot Italian), cut into ½ inch (12 mm) pieces	1 lb.	454 g
Lean pork, cut bite size	1½ lbs.	680 g
Long grain white rice, uncooked	1½ cups	375 mL
Chopped onion	1 cup	250 mL
Chopped celery	⅓ cup	75 mL
Water	3½ cups	875 mL
Salsa	½ cup	125 mL
Beef bouillon powder	1 tbsp.	15 mL
Cayenne pepper	½ tsp.	2 mL
Garlic powder	¼ tsp.	1 mL
Salt	½ tsp.	2 mL
Pepper	¼ tsp.	1 mL

Brown sausage pieces on medium-high heat in pressure cooker. Add pork. Stir and cook for 1 to 2 minutes until firm. Drain.

Pour rice evenly over meat. Scatter onion and celery over rice.

Mix remaining 7 ingredients in medium bowl. Pour over all. Secure lid. Bring up to pressure on high heat. Reduce heat to medium. Cook for 15 minutes. Remove from heat. Let pressure drop on its own. Remove lid. Serves 8 to 10.

1 serving: 509 Calories; 24.2 g Total Fat; 1385 mg Sodium; 35 g Protein; 35 g Carbohydrate; 1 g Dietary Fiber

Pictured on page 107.

Paré Pointer

The moths ate the rug so they could see the floor.

Holiday Pudding

Good rich flavor — and in just over one hour compared with three hours for regular steaming. Serve with your favorite hard sauce or rum sauce.

Granulated sugar	½ cup	125 mL
Dry fine bread crumbs	½ cup	125 mL
All-purpose flour	1 cup	250 mL
Baking powder	1½ tsp.	7 mL
Baking soda	½ tsp.	2 mL
Ground cinnamon	1 tsp.	5 mL
Ground allspice	½ tsp.	2 mL
Ground cardamom	⅛ tsp.	0.5 mL
Salt	½ tsp.	2 mL
Hard margarine (or butter)	½ cup	125 mL
Raisins	½ cup	125 mL
Cut glazed mixed fruit	½ cup	125 mL
Chopped dates	½ cup	125 mL
Chopped walnuts	½ cup	125 mL
Large eggs	2	2
Prepared orange juice	1 cup	250 mL
Water	4 cups	1 L

Measure first 9 ingredients into large bowl. Cut in margarine until crumbly.

Add raisins, fruit, dates and walnuts. Stir.

Beat eggs in small bowl. Add orange juice. Stir. Mix into dry ingredients. Grease 8 cup (2 L) metal bowl. Bowl should not fit too tightly in cooker. Turn pudding into bowl. Cover with foil. Tie with string.

Pour water into pressure cooker. Add rack. Set bowl on rack in cooker. Secure lid. Bring up to pressure on high heat. Reduce heat to medium. Cook for 75 minutes. Remove from heat. Let pressure drop on its own. Remove lid. Serve warm. Makes a 2 lb. (900 g) pudding. Serves 8.

1 serving: 433 Calories; 19.2 g Total Fat; 482 mg Sodium; 6 g Protein; 62 g Carbohydrate; 3 g Dietary Fiber

Bread Pudding

Brings a bit of nostalgia to most folks.

Cubed day-old French bread	4 cups	1 L
Milk	3 cups	750 mL
Raisins	½ cup	125 mL
Large eggs	4	4
Granulated sugar	1 cup	250 mL
Vanilla	2 tsp.	10 mL
Ground cinnamon	½ tsp.	2 mL
Ground nutmeg	¼ tsp.	1 mL
Ground allspice	¼ tsp.	1 mL
Salt	¼ tsp.	1 mL
Water	1½ cups	375 mL

Combine bread, milk and raisins in large bowl. Press bread into milk.

Beat eggs in medium bowl until frothy. Beat in sugar. Add vanilla, cinnamon, nutmeg, allspice and salt. Beat well. Add to bread mixture. Stir well. Turn into greased 8 cup (2 L) metal mold. Cover with waxed paper.

Pour water into pressure cooker. Set rack in bottom. Place pudding on rack. Secure lid. Bring up to pressure on high heat. Reduce heat to medium. Cook for 18 minutes. Remove from heat. Let pressure drop on its own. Remove lid. Serves 8.

1 serving: 258 Calories; 4.1 g Total Fat; 257 mg Sodium; 8 g Protein; 48 g Carbohydrate; 1 g Dietary Fiber

1. Pork Jambalaya, page 104
   (Pressure Cooker)
2. Vegetable Beef Soup, page 94
   (Pressure Cooker)
3. Chicken Cacciatore, page 98
   (Pressure Cooker)
4. Navy Bean Soup, page 94
   (Pressure Cooker)

Props Courtesy Of: Le Gnome
Stokes

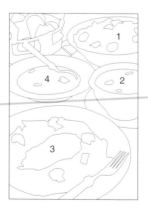

Chocolate Pudding Cake

*Serve this with your favorite chocolate sauce or with a
dollop of whipped topping.*

Hard margarine (or butter), softened	¼ cup	60 mL
Granulated sugar	¾ cup	175 mL
Large egg	1	1
Milk	¾ cup	175 mL
All-purpose flour	2 cups	500 mL
Cocoa, sifted if lumpy	¼ cup	60 mL
Baking powder	1 tbsp.	15 mL
Vanilla	1 tsp.	5 mL
Salt	½ tsp.	2 mL
Water	1½ cups	375 mL

Cream margarine and sugar in large bowl. Beat in egg. Add milk.
Beat slowly.

Add remaining 5 ingredients. Beat on low just until moistened. Turn into
greased 8 cup (2 L) metal pan. Tie foil over top.

Pour water into pressure cooker. Set rack in bottom. Place cake on rack.
Secure lid. Bring up to pressure on high heat. Reduce heat to medium.
Cook for 45 minutes. Remove from heat. Let pressure drop on its own.
Remove lid. Makes 8 servings.

*1 serving: 281 Calories; 7.6 g Total Fat; 269 mg Sodium; 6 g Protein; 49 g Carbohydrate;
2 g Dietary Fiber*

Pictured on page 90.

1. Hot Tuna Sandwiches, page 114
   (Sandwich Maker)
2. S'more Toasts, page 120
   (Sandwich Maker)
3. Lunchtime Tater Cakes, page 116
   (Sandwich Maker)
4. Chili Snacks, page 115
   (Sandwich Maker)

Props Courtesy Of: The Bay
                     Zenari's

Spicy Stuffed Apples

The stuffing is "oh-so-good!" Drizzle with a little cream for a very special treat.

Chopped dried apricots	¼ cup	60 mL
Orange-flavored liqueur (such as Grand Marnier or Triple Sec), or orange juice	¼ cup	60 mL
Chopped walnuts	¼ cup	60 mL
Brown sugar, packed	2 tbsp.	30 mL
Grated orange peel (optional)	½ tsp.	2 mL
Ground ginger	¼ tsp.	1 mL
Ground cardamom	¼ tsp.	1 mL
Ground cinnamon	¼ tsp.	1 mL
Ground nutmeg	⅛ tsp.	0.5 mL
Medium cooking apples (such as McIntosh), about 1 lb. (454 g)	4	4
Margarine (or butter)	4 tsp.	20 mL
Water	½ cup	125 mL

Soak apricots in liqueur in small bowl for 15 minutes until liquid is absorbed.

Add next 7 ingredients. Stir.

Core apples most of the way through, leaving bottoms still intact. Peel away skins about ⅓ of the way down apple. Stuff each apple with ¼ of apricot mixture. Dot each with 1 tsp. (5 mL) margarine. Place each apple on 12 x 12 inch (30 x 30 cm) square of foil and bring up all sides. Twist foil to secure tightly at top.

Pour water into pressure cooker. Set rack in bottom. Place covered apples on rack. Secure lid. Bring up to pressure on high heat. Reduce heat to medium. Cook for 10 minutes. Remove from heat. Cool cooker under cold running water to reduce pressure quickly. Remove lid. Carefully unwrap apples. Serves 4.

1 serving: 265 Calories; 9.6 g Total Fat; 51 mg Sodium; 2 g Protein; 37 g Carbohydrate; 3 g Dietary Fiber

Caramel Pecan Cheesecake

A decadent topping of caramel and nuts.

Caramel sundae topping	⅓ cup	75 mL
Chopped pecans, toasted	2 tbsp.	30 mL
Cream cheese, softened	12 oz.	375 g
Brown sugar, packed	½ cup	125 mL
Large eggs	2	2
Margarine (or butter), melted	2 tbsp.	30 mL
Graham cracker crumbs	½ cup	125 mL
Water	2½ cups	625 mL

Line 6 inch (15 cm) ceramic soufflé dish with aluminum foil. Press foil inside to make smooth. Pour in caramel topping to cover bottom. Sprinkle with pecans.

Beat cream cheese and brown sugar until smooth. Add eggs, 1 at a time, beating well on low speed after each addition. Pour over pecans.

Combine melted margarine with graham crumbs in small bowl. Sprinkle evenly over surface of cheesecake. Cover dish with aluminum foil. Tie with string to secure foil.

Pour water into pressure cooker. Set rack in bottom. Place cheesecake on rack. Secure lid. Bring up to pressure on high heat. Reduce heat to medium. Cook for 40 minutes. Remove from heat. Let pressure drop on its own. Remove lid. Remove dish. Remove foil cover. Cool in baking dish on a wire rack. Invert onto serving plate. Carefully peel off foil. Serves 8.

1 serving: 311 Calories; 20.7 g Total Fat; 225 mg Sodium; 6 g Protein; 27 g Carbohydrate; trace Dietary Fiber

 Hard block margarine produces the best results in the sandwich maker. Soft tub (regular or diet) margarine will produce soggy sandwiches because of their increased water content.

White Fruitcake

Heavy and dense with fruit. Good apricot and raisin flavor.

Glazed cherries	½ cup	125 mL
Golden raisins	1 cup	250 mL
Chopped dried apricots	½ cup	125 mL
Chopped dates	½ cup	125 mL
Chopped almonds	1 cup	250 mL
All-purpose flour	¼ cup	60 mL
Hard margarine (or butter), softened	½ cup	125 mL
Granulated sugar	½ cup	125 mL
Large eggs	4	4
Vanilla	½ tsp.	2 mL
Almond flavoring	½ tsp.	2 mL
Pineapple juice	⅓ cup	75 mL
All-purpose flour	1 cup	250 mL
Baking powder	1 tsp.	5 mL
Salt	½ tsp.	2 mL
Water	4 cups	1 L

Put first 6 ingredients into medium bowl. Stir well to coat with flour.

Cream margarine and sugar in large bowl. Beat in eggs, 1 at a time. Add vanilla, almond flavoring and pineapple juice. Mix.

Stir flour, baking powder and salt together in small bowl. Add to batter. Stir just to moisten. Add fruit mixture. Stir. Line greased 8 cup (2 L) metal pudding mold with waxed paper. Mold should not fit too tightly into pressure cooker. Turn cake batter into mold. Cover with foil. Secure foil with string.

Set rack in bottom of pressure cooker. Add water. Set mold on rack. Cover. Secure lid. Bring up to pressure on high heat. Reduce heat to medium. Cook for 90 minutes. Remove from heat. Let pressure drop on its own. Remove lid. Cool in pan. Turn cake out and remove waxed paper. Makes a 2½ lb. (1.1 kg) cake. Cuts into 24 pieces.

1 piece: 174 Calories; 7.9 g Total Fat; 117 mg Sodium; 3 g Protein; 24 g Carbohydrate; 2 g Dietary Fiber

Pictured on page 90.

Dark Fruitcake

Cover the top of this cake with a thick layer of marzipan for an old fashioned look.

Glazed cherries, quartered	½ cup	125 mL
Cut glazed mixed peel	¼ cup	60 mL
Raisins	1 cup	250 mL
Chopped candied pineapple	½ cup	125 mL
Coarsely chopped pecans	½ cup	125 mL
All-purpose flour	¼ cup	60 mL
Hard margarine (or butter), softened	½ cup	125 mL
Brown sugar, packed	1 cup	250 mL
Large eggs	5	5
Prepared orange juice	⅓ cup	75 mL
All-purpose flour	1½ cups	375 mL
Baking powder	1¼ tsp.	6 mL
Ground cinnamon	1¼ tsp.	6 mL
Ground allspice	½ tsp.	2 mL
Ground cloves	¼ tsp.	1 mL
Salt	½ tsp.	2 mL
Water	4 cups	1 L

Put first 6 ingredients into medium bowl. Stir well to coat with flour.

Cream margarine and brown sugar in large bowl. Beat in eggs, 1 at a time. Add orange juice. Beat.

Stir remaining 6 ingredients together in small bowl. Add to batter. Stir just to moisten. Add fruit mixture. Stir. Line greased 8 cup (2 L) metal mold with waxed paper. Mold should not fit too tightly into pressure cooker. Turn cake batter into mold. Cover with foil. Secure foil with string.

Set rack in bottom of pressure cooker. Add water. Place mold on rack. Secure lid. Bring up to pressure on high heat. Reduce heat to medium. Cook for 90 minutes. Remove from heat. Let pressure drop on its own. Remove lid. Cool in pan. Turn cake out and remove waxed paper. Makes a 2¾ lb.(1.25 kg) cake. Cuts into 24 pieces.

1 piece: 195 Calories; 7 g Total Fat; 123 mg Sodium; 3 g Protein; 31 g Carbohydrate; 1 g Dietary Fiber

Sandwich Maker

The sandwich maker used for testing was a model that holds two sandwiches, making a total of four triangles. With only one temperature, the indicator light came on when the machine was ready. Read your owner's manual to learn your model's features and limitations.

Hot Tuna Sandwiches

Such good tasting sandwiches. Refrigerate unused filling for up to 3 days.

Can of white tuna, packed in water, drained and broken into chunks	6 oz.	170 g
Hard-boiled eggs, chopped	2	2
Grated sharp Cheddar cheese	⅔ cup	150 mL
Finely chopped green onion	2 tbsp.	30 mL
Finely chopped celery	2 tbsp.	30 mL
Can of condensed cream of mushroom soup (10 oz., 284 mL)	½	½
Salt	½ tsp.	2 mL
Pepper	⅟₁₆ tsp.	0.5 mL
Hard margarine (or butter), softened	⅓ cup	75 mL
White (or whole wheat) bread slices	16	16

Mix first 8 ingredients in medium bowl.

Spread margarine on 1 side of each bread slice. Spread each of 8 unbuttered sides with ¼ cup (60 mL) tuna mixture. Cover with remaining 8 slices, unbuttered side down. Place, 2 at a time, in preheated sandwich maker. Close lid. Toast for 3 to 4 minutes until browned. Makes 16 triangles.

1 triangle: 164 Calories; 8.2 g Total Fat; 425 mg Sodium; 7 g Protein; 15 g Carbohydrate; 1 g Dietary Fiber

Pictured on page 108.

Chili Snacks

Make these up ahead of time and reheat when needed or keep filling chilled to make as needed. Add a few fresh veggies and lunch is ready!

Light cream cheese, softened	4 oz.	125 g
Chili with beans (your own or canned)	½ cup	125 mL
Hard margarine (or butter), softened	⅓ cup	75 mL
White (or whole wheat) bread slices	16	16

Mix cheese and chili in small bowl.

Spread margarine on 1 side of each bread slice. Spread each of 8 unbuttered sides with 2 tbsp. (30 mL) chili mixture. Cover with remaining 8 slices, unbuttered side down. Place in preheated sandwich maker. Close lid. Toast for about 2 to 3 minutes until golden. Makes 16 triangles.

1 triangle: 136 Calories; 6.6 g Total Fat; 301 mg Sodium; 4 g Protein; 15 g Carbohydrate; 1 g Dietary Fiber

Pictured on page 108.

Spaghetti Sandwich

A great way to use leftover spaghetti and sauce.

Hard margarine (or butter), softened	2 tbsp.	30 mL
Garlic powder	⅟₁₆ tsp.	0.5 mL
Dried whole oregano	⅟₁₆ tsp.	0.5 mL
White (or whole wheat) sandwich bread slices	4	4
Cold leftover cooked spaghetti, with sauce	1 cup	250 mL
Grated Parmesan cheese	2 tsp.	10 mL

Combine margarine with garlic powder and oregano in small dish.

Spread on 1 side of each bread slice.

Spread each of 2 unbuttered sides with ½ cup (125 mL) spaghetti mixture. Sprinkle Parmesan cheese over spaghetti mixture. Cover with remaining 2 bread slices, unbuttered side down. Place in preheated sandwich maker. Close lid. Toast for 5 minutes until browned. Makes 4 triangles.

1 triangle: 219 Calories; 10 g Total Fat; 505 mg Sodium; 8 g Protein; 24 g Carbohydrate; 1 g Dietary Fiber

Lunchtime Tater Cakes

Different way to use your sandwich maker. Serve with applesauce or sour cream.

Medium baking potato (about 6 oz., 170 g), peeled and grated	1	1
Chopped green onion	2 tbsp.	30 mL
Large egg, fork-beaten	1	1
Margarine (or butter), melted	2 tsp.	10 mL
All-purpose flour	1 tbsp.	15 mL
Baking powder	¼ tsp.	1 mL
Salt	¼ tsp.	¼ tsp.
Bacon slice, cooked crisp and crumbled (or 1 tbsp., 15 mL, real bacon bits), optional	1	1

Combine all 8 ingredients in small bowl. Spray sandwich maker with no-stick cooking spray. Spoon about ¼ cup (60 mL) potato mixture into each depression of preheated sandwich maker. Close lid. Cook for 15 to 20 minutes until potatoes are cooked and browned. Makes 4.

1 tater cake: 65 Calories; 3.1 g Total Fat; 210 mg Sodium; 2 g Protein; 7 g Carbohydrate; 1 g Dietary Fiber

Pictured on page 108.

Crabby Packets

Nicely filled golden brown triangles.

Light cream cheese, softened	4 oz.	125 g
Worcestershire sauce	1 tsp.	5 mL
Lemon juice	1 tsp.	5 mL
Minced onion flakes	1 tbsp.	15 mL
Milk	1½ tbsp.	25 mL
Hot pepper sauce	¹⁄₁₆ tsp.	0.5 mL
Can of crabmeat, drained, cartilage removed, flaked	4.2 oz.	120 g
Hard margarine (or butter), softened	8 tsp.	40 mL
White (or whole wheat) bread slices	8	8

(continued on next page)

116   Sandwich Maker

Beat first 6 ingredients in medium bowl until smooth.

Stir in crabmeat.

Spread margarine on 1 side of each bread slice. Spread each of 4 unbuttered sides with ¼ cup (60 mL) crab mixture. Cover with remaining 4 slices, unbuttered side down. Place in preheated sandwich maker. Close lid. Toast for 2 minutes. Makes 8 triangles.

1 triangle: 154 Calories; 7.3 g Total Fat; 429 mg Sodium; 6 g Protein; 16 g Carbohydrate; 1 g Dietary Fiber

Corn Fritters

*Dip in strawberry jam or honey for a real treat
or serve hot with butter and syrup.*

All-purpose flour	⅔ cup	150 mL
Cornmeal	⅓ cup	75 mL
Granulated sugar	1 tbsp.	15 mL
Baking powder	1½ tsp.	7 mL
Salt	½ tsp.	2 mL
Large egg, fork-beaten	1	1
Margarine (or butter), melted	2 tbsp.	30 mL
Milk	¼ cup	60 mL

Combine first 5 ingredients in medium bowl. Make a well.

Add next 3 ingredients to well in order given. Mix just until flour is moistened. Spray sandwich maker with no-stick cooking spray. Spoon about ¼ cup (60 mL) batter into each depression of preheated sandwich maker. Close lid. Cook for 5 minutes until golden. Makes 5 fritters.

1 fritter: 170 Calories; 5.8 g Total Fat; 346 mg Sodium; 4 g Protein; 25 g Carbohydrate; 1 g Dietary Fiber

Monte Cristo Sandwich

A favorite sandwich done up in a different style.

Grated Swiss cheese	2 tbsp.	30 mL
White (or whole wheat) sandwich bread slices	4	4
Ham, deli thin slices, chopped or cut into strips	1½ oz.	42 g
White turkey, deli thin slices, chopped or cut into strips	1½ oz.	42 g
Freshly ground pepper, sprinkle		
Large eggs, fork-beaten	2	2
Water	2 tbsp.	30 mL

Divide and sprinkle first amount of cheese on 2 bread slices.

Divide ham and turkey over cheese. Sprinkle with pepper. Divide and sprinkle second amount of cheese over meat. Cover with remaining 2 bread slices.

Spray preheated sandwich maker with no-stick cooking spray. Combine eggs and water with fork in 9 inch (22 cm) pie plate. Hold each sandwich firmly together on sides and dip top and bottom into egg mixture. Place in sandwich maker. Close lid. Toast for about 5 minutes until browned. Makes 4 triangles.

1 triangle: 168 Calories; 6.5 g Total Fat; 431 mg Sodium; 12 g Protein; 15 g Carbohydrate; 1 g Dietary Fiber

Pictured on front cover.

Mince Pie Singles

This tasty dessert is so quick to make.

Mincemeat	2 tbsp.	30 mL
Applesauce	2 tbsp.	30 mL
Cornstarch	1/16 tsp.	0.5 mL

(continued on next page)

| Hard margarine (or butter), softened | 4 tsp. | 20 mL |
| Raisin (or white) bread slices | 4 | 4 |

Stir mincemeat, applesauce and cornstarch together well in small cup.

Spread margarine on 1 side of each bread slice. Drop 2 tbsp. (30 mL) mincemeat mixture onto center of 2 unbuttered sides. Cover with remaining 2 slices, unbuttered sides down. Place in preheated sandwich maker. Close lid. Toast for 2 minutes until golden. Makes 4 triangles.

1 triangle: 121 Calories; 4.8 g Total Fat; 154 mg Sodium; 2 g Protein; 18 g Carbohydrate; 1 g Dietary Fiber

Raisin Pies

Flaky golden pockets full of sweet raisins.

Raisins	1 cup	250 mL
Water	½ cup	125 mL
Brown sugar, packed	¼ cup	60 mL
All-purpose flour	2 tbsp.	30 mL
Lemon juice	2 tsp.	10 mL
Vanilla	¼ tsp.	1 mL
Phyllo pastry sheets	4	4
Hard margarine (or butter), melted	2 tbsp.	30 mL

Measure raisins and water into small saucepan. Cover. Simmer for 5 minutes.

Mix brown sugar and flour in cup. Stir into raisin mixture until boiling and thickened. Stir in lemon juice and vanilla. Cool.

Lay 1 sheet of phyllo on working surface. Cover remaining sheets with damp cloth. Brush top side of sheet with margarine. Fold into thirds. Brush top and bottom sides with margarine. Fold in all 4 sides so pastry will just fit into sandwich maker. Repeat with remaining 3 sheets of phyllo. Place 1 folded sheet in preheated sandwich maker. Put 2 tbsp. (30 mL) filling into each depression. Cover with second folded sheet. Close lid. Toast for 4 minutes until pastry is golden. Repeat with remaining 2 folded sheets and remaining filling. Makes 8 triangles.

1 triangle: 153 Calories; 3 g Total Fat; 104 mg Sodium; 2 g Protein; 31 g Carbohydrate; 1 g Dietary Fiber

Banana Toasties

Bound to be a favorite of kids.

Hard margarine (or butter), softened	4 tsp.	20 mL
White (or whole wheat) bread slices	4	4
Brown sugar, packed	4 tsp.	20 mL
Semisweet chocolate chips	2 tsp.	10 mL
Diced banana	¼ cup	60 mL

Spread margarine on 1 side of each bread slice.

Sprinkle 2 tsp. (10 mL) brown sugar on unbuttered side of 2 slices.

Sprinkle chocolate chips over sugar. Scatter diced banana over chips. Top with remaining 2 bread slices, unbuttered side down. Place in preheated sandwich maker. Close lid. Toast for about 2 minutes. Makes 4 triangles.

1 triangle: 142 Calories; 5.4 g Total Fat; 189 mg Sodium; 3 g Protein; 21 g Carbohydrate; 1 g Dietary Fiber

S'more Toasts

A real sweet treat to be sure. Be careful of the hot filling with smaller children.

Hard margarine (or butter), softened	4 tsp.	20 mL
White (or whole wheat) bread slices	4	4
Graham cracker crumbs	4 tsp.	20 mL
Miniature marshmallows	40	40
Semisweet chocolate chips	4 tsp.	20 mL
Graham cracker crumbs	2 tbsp.	30 mL

Spread margarine on 1 side of each bread slice. Sprinkle with 1 tsp. (5 mL) graham crumbs.

(continued on next page)

Carefully turn over 2 bread slices. Divide marshmallows between 2 unbuttered sides. Divide and sprinkle chocolate chips over marshmallows. Sprinkle with remaining graham crumbs. Top with remaining 2 slices of bread, unbuttered side down. Place in preheated sandwich maker. Close lid. Toast for about 2 minutes until browned. Makes 4 triangles.

1 triangle: 175 Calories; 6.3 g Total Fat; 240 mg Sodium; 3 g Protein; 27 g Carbohydrate; 1 g Dietary Fiber

Pictured on page 108.

Berry Cheesy Sweet

Very tasty. Browned sandwich triangles with a creamy fruit filling.

Hard margarine (or butter), softened	4 tsp.	20 mL
White (or whole wheat) bread slices	4	4
Spreadable cream cheese	3 tbsp.	50 mL
Granulated sugar	1 tbsp.	15 mL
Vanilla	⅛ tsp.	0.5 mL
Diced fresh (or frozen, thawed) strawberries	¼ cup	60 mL

Spread margarine on 1 side of each bread slice.

Mash cream cheese, sugar and vanilla with fork on medium plate. Spread on unbuttered sides of 4 bread slices, keeping in ¼ inch (6 mm) from edge.

Scatter dried strawberries over cream cheese mixture on 2 slices. Cover with remaining bread slices, cream cheese mixture down. Place in preheated sandwich maker. Close lid. Toast for about 2 minutes until browned. Makes 4 triangles.

1 triangle: 164 Calories; 8.7 g Total Fat; 221 mg Sodium; 3 g Protein; 18 g Carbohydrate; 1 g Dietary Fiber

Slow Cooker

We tested our recipes with a 3½ quart (3.5 L), 4½ quart (4.5 L), 6½ quart (6.5 L) slow cooker. All had High and Low temperature settings. Read your owner's manual to learn your model's features and limitations. Some newer models feature a kitchen-to-table removable crock or liner, in a variety of designer colors.

Boston Brown Bread

Bostonians would love this served warm with butter.

Cornmeal	1 cup	250 mL
Whole wheat flour	1½ cups	375 mL
All-purpose flour	½ cup	125 mL
Baking soda	1½ tsp.	7 mL
Salt	1 tsp.	5 mL
Fancy (mild) molasses	¾ cup	175 mL
Water	1 cup	250 mL
Buttermilk (or reconstituted from powder)	1 cup	250 mL

Measure first 5 ingredients into large bowl.

Mix molasses and water in medium bowl until smooth. Add buttermilk. Stir. Add to flour mixture. Stir just to moisten. Turn into greased 3½ quart (3.5 L) slow cooker. Place 5 paper towels between top of slow cooker and lid. Put wooden match or an object ⅛ inch (3 mm) thick between paper towels and edge of slow cooker to allow a bit of steam to escape. Do not lift lid for first 1¾ hours of cooking time. Cook on High for about 2½ to 3 hours until wooden pick inserted in center of bread comes out clean. Loosen sides with knife. Turn out onto wire rack to cool. Cuts into 18 slices.

1 slice: 121 Calories; 0.5 g Total Fat; 283 mg Sodium; 3 g Protein; 27 g Carbohydrate; 2 g Dietary Fiber

Pictured on page 35 and on back cover.

Oriental Snack Mix

Crisp, lightly seasoned munchies.

Unsweetened corn and rice squares cereal (such as Crispix)	2½ cups	625 mL
Package of crisp chow mein noodles (6 oz., 170 g)	½	½
Slivered almonds	½ cup	125 mL
Package of Oriental noodle soup, broken up (flavor packet discarded or saved for fried rice)	3½ oz.	100 g
Blanched unsalted peanuts	½ cup	125 mL
Unsalted butter (not margarine)	¼ cup	60 mL
Light soy sauce	3 tbsp.	50 mL
Ground ginger	½ tsp.	2 mL
Garlic powder	¼ tsp.	1 mL
Onion powder	¼ tsp.	1 mL
Cayenne pepper	⅛ tsp.	0.5 mL
Brown sugar, packed	1½ tsp.	7 mL

Combine first 5 ingredients in 4½ quart (4.5 L) slow cooker.

Melt butter in small saucepan. Stir in remaining 6 ingredients. Pour over cereal mixture in slow cooker. Stir and toss well to coat. Cook on Low for 2 hours, stirring occasionally, until crisp and golden. Cool. Store in sealed container. Makes 4½ cups (1.1 L).

½ cup (125 mL): 553 Calories; 34 g Total Fat; 941 mg Sodium; 14 g Protein; 52 g Carbohydrate; 4 g Dietary Fiber

Pictured on page 143.

Paré Pointer

The duck paid to get in; he had a bill.
The frog had a green back but the skunk only had a scent.

Make-Ahead Potatoes

A great way to have part of your meal ready and waiting.

Medium potatoes, peeled and quartered	9	9
Water		
Package of light cream cheese, softened and cut up	8 oz.	250 g
Light sour cream	1 cup	250 mL
Onion powder	½ tsp.	2 mL
Garlic powder	¼ tsp.	1 mL
Parsley flakes	1 tsp.	5 mL
Chopped chives	1 tbsp.	15 mL
Salt	1 tsp.	5 mL
Pepper	¼ tsp.	1 mL

Cook potatoes in water in large pot or Dutch oven until tender. Drain. Mash.

Measure remaining 8 ingredients into medium bowl. Beat until well blended. Add to potatoes. Mix well. Turn into 3½ quart (3.5 L) slow cooker. Chill if using next day. Cook on Low for 6 to 8 hours or on High, stirring occasionally, for 3 to 4 hours. Makes 8 cups (2 L).

1 cup (250 mL): 192 Calories; 7.5 g Total Fat; 658 mg Sodium; 7 g Protein; 25 g Carbohydrate; 2 g Dietary Fiber

1. Steak Bake, page 131
   (Slow Cooker)
2. Chinese Pepper Steak, page 130
   (Slow Cooker)
3. Beefy Bun Topping, page 129
   (Slow Cooker)

Props Courtesy Of: Proctor-Silex
Zenari's

Slow Cooker

Dressed Red Potatoes

A full-of-flavor potato that's a snap to make.

Unpeeled small red potatoes, halved	2½ lbs.	1.1 kg
Package of light cream cheese, softened	8 oz.	225 g
Can of condensed cream of potato soup	10 oz.	284 mL
Envelope of buttermilk dill (or ranch) dressing mix	1 oz.	28 g
Parsley flakes	1 tsp.	5 mL

Put potatoes in bottom of 3½ quart (3.5 L) slow cooker.

Beat cream cheese and potato soup in medium bowl. Beat in dressing mix and parsley. Spoon over potatoes. Cover. Cook on Low for 6 to 7 hours or on High for 3 to 3½ hours. Makes 9½ cups (2.4 L).

1 cup (250 mL): 163 Calories; 4.7 g Total Fat; 699 mg Sodium; 6 g Protein; 25 g Carbohydrate; 2 g Dietary Fiber

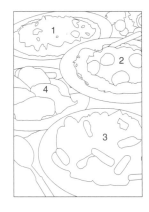

1. Teriyaki Steak, page 132 **(Slow Cooker)**
2. Spaghetti Sauce And Meatballs, page 128 **(Slow Cooker)**
3. Beef Bourguignon, page 134 **(Slow Cooker)**
4. Chicken Parmigiana, page 136 **(Slow Cooker)**

Props Courtesy Of: The Bay

Spaghetti Sauce And Meatballs

It's the parmesan that makes these meatballs delicious.
Garnish with fresh grated Parmesan for extra delicious!

Chopped onion	1 cup	250 mL
Garlic cloves, minced	2	2
Olive oil	1 tbsp.	15 mL
SAUCE		
Can of roma (plum) tomatoes, with juice, mashed	28 oz.	796 mL
Can of tomato sauce	7½ oz.	213 mL
Can of tomato paste	5½ oz.	156 mL
Dry (or alcohol-free) red wine	¼ cup	60 mL
Dried sweet basil	2 tsp.	10 mL
Dried whole oregano	1 tsp.	5 mL
Dried rosemary, crushed	1 tsp.	5 mL
Granulated sugar	1 tsp.	5 mL
Cayenne pepper	⅛ tsp.	0.5 mL
MEATBALLS		
Fine dry bread crumbs	¼ cup	60 mL
Milk	¼ cup	60 mL
Large egg, fork-beaten	1	1
Grated Parmesan cheese	¼ cup	60 mL
Parsley flakes	1 tsp.	5 mL
Onion powder	½ tsp.	2 mL
Freshly ground pepper, sprinkle		
Extra lean ground beef	1 lb.	454 g

Sauté onion and garlic in olive oil in frying pan until softened. Turn into 6½ quart (6.5 L) slow cooker.

Sauce: Add all 9 sauce ingredients to onion mixture. Stir.

(continued on next page)

Meatballs: Mix first 7 ingredients in medium bowl. Let for stand 5 minutes.

Add ground beef. Stir well to combine. Form mixture into twenty 1½ inch (3.8 cm) balls. Add to sauce. Cover. Cook on Low for 7 to 8 hours or on High for 3½ to 4 hours. Makes about 5 cups (1.25 L) sauce and 20 meatballs. Serves 4.

1 serving: 516 Calories; 24.6 g Total Fat; 975 mg Sodium; 40 g Protein; 34 g Carbohydrate; 6 g Dietary Fiber

Pictured on page 126.

Beefy Bun Topping

Serve on open-faced toasted hamburger buns. Add cucumber and tomatoes for color and for added nutrition. Keep in the freezer for emergencies.

Extra lean ground beef	2 lbs.	900 g
Large onion, chopped	1	1
Can of tomato paste	5½ oz.	156 mL
Can of tomatoes, with juice	14 oz.	398 mL
Beef bouillon powder	2 tsp.	10 mL
Dry mustard	½ tsp.	2 mL
Brown sugar, packed	1½ tbsp.	25 mL
Pepper	¼ tsp.	1 mL
Chili powder	1 tbsp.	15 mL

Brown ground beef in non-stick frying pan until no pink remains. Drain.

Add onion. Stir. Turn into 3½ quart (3.5 L) slow cooker.

Stir remaining 7 ingredients in medium bowl. Pour over beef mixture. Stir. Cover. Cook on Low for 5 to 6 hours or on High for 2½ to 3 hours. Makes 6 cups (1.5 L).

½ cup (125 mL): 149 Calories; 6.9 g Total Fat; 209 mg Sodium; 15 g Protein; 7 g Carbohydrate; 1 g Dietary Fiber

Pictured on page 125.

 Protect the crock liner of your slow cooker by avoiding sudden temperature changes. Don't place a hot crock in cold water or on a wet surface.

Chinese Pepper Steak

A super combination of all things good.
Serve over long grain white rice or aromatic basmati rice.

Large onion, thinly sliced	1	1
Cooking oil	1 tbsp.	15 mL
Beef round steak, cut into strips	2 lbs.	900 g
Beef bouillon powder	1 tsp.	5 mL
Granulated sugar	1 tsp.	5 mL
Garlic powder (or 1 garlic clove, minced)	¼ tsp.	1 mL
Salt	¾ tsp.	4 mL
Pepper	⅛ tsp.	0.5 mL
Can of diced tomatoes, with juice	14 oz.	398 mL
Soy sauce	¼ cup	60 mL
Fresh bean sprouts	1½ cups	375 mL
Green pepper, slivered	1	1
Red pepper, slivered	1	1
Fresh pea pods (about 2 oz., 57 g)	1½ cups	375 mL
Cornstarch	2 tbsp.	30 mL
Water	3 tbsp.	50 mL

Layer onion slices in bottom of 3½ quart (3.5 L) slow cooker.

Heat cooking oil in frying pan on medium-high. Brown steak strips until no longer pink. Layer over onions.

Stir next 7 ingredients together in medium bowl. Pour over steak. Cover. Cook on Low for 6 to 7 hours or on High for 3 to 3½ hours.

Add next 4 ingredients. Stir.

Combine cornstarch and water in small dish. Stir into steak mixture. Cover. Cook on High for 15 minutes until vegetables are tender crisp and liquid is slightly thickened. Makes 9 cups (2.25 L).

1 cup (250 mL): 196 Calories; 5.5 g Total Fat; 912 mg Sodium; 26 g Protein; 10 g Carbohydrate; 2 g Dietary Fiber

Pictured on page 125.

Steak Bake

So tender and economical, you can enjoy this steak often. Serve with rice.

Medium onion, sliced	1	1
Medium potatoes, peeled and quartered	4	4
Medium carrots, sliced	4	4
Beef round steak, cut into 8 pieces	1¼ lbs.	560 g
Can of diced tomatoes, with juice	14 oz.	398 mL
Can of condensed tomato soup	10 oz.	284 mL
Garlic powder	¼ tsp.	1 mL
Salt	1 tsp.	5 mL
Pepper	¼ tsp.	1 mL
Liquid gravy browner (such as Kitchen Bouquet)	½ tsp.	2 mL
Can of cut green beans, drained	14 oz.	398 mL
All-purpose flour (optional)	2 tbsp.	30 mL
Liquid from slow cooker (optional)	¼ cup	60 mL
Chopped green onion, for garnish		

Layer first 4 ingredients in bottom of 3½ quart (3.5 L) slow cooker in order listed.

Mix next 6 ingredients in medium bowl. Pour over steak.

Scatter green beans over top. Cover. Cook on Low for 8 to 10 hours or on High for 4 to 5 hours.

To thicken slightly, mix flour and liquid until smooth. Stir into steak mixture. Cook on High for 15 minutes. Garnish with green onion. Serves 4.

1 serving: 254 Calories; 3.1 g Total Fat; 1074 mg Sodium; 26 g Protein; 32 g Carbohydrate; 5 g Dietary Fiber

Pictured on page 131.

Paré Pointer

A squirrel's nest is better known as a nutcracker suite.

Curried Beef

Lots of saucy fruit and beef to serve over rice.

Beef stew meat, cubed	2½ lbs.	1.1 kg
All-purpose flour	⅓ cup	75 mL
Cooking oil	1 tbsp.	15 mL
Can of crushed pineapple, drained	14 oz.	398 mL
Can of tomato sauce	14 oz.	398 mL
Can of sliced peaches, with juice	14 oz.	398 mL
Medium onion, chopped	1	1
Raisins	½ cup	125 mL
Garlic clove, minced (or ¼ tsp., 1 mL, garlic powder)	1	1
Beef bouillon powder	1 tbsp.	15 mL
Curry powder	2 tsp.	10 mL
Pepper	¼ tsp.	1 mL
Ground cardamom	⅛ tsp.	0.5 mL
Ground coriander	⅛ tsp.	0.5 mL
Ground cumin	⅛ tsp.	0.5 mL

Coat beef with flour. Heat cooking oil in frying pan on medium-high. Brown beef until no longer pink. Turn into 3½ quart (3.5 L) slow cooker.

Mix next 12 ingredients in large bowl. Stir. Pour over beef. Cover. Cook on Low for 8 to 10 hours or on High for 4 to 5 hours. Makes 8 cups (2 L).

1 cup (250 mL): 386 Calories; 14.4 g Total Fat; 623 mg Sodium; 33 g Protein; 32 g Carbohydrate; 3 g Dietary Fiber

Meatballs In Gravy

This pleases everybody. Serve over noodles.

Finely chopped onion	¼ cup	60 mL
Dry bread crumbs	½ cup	125 mL
Pepper	¼ tsp.	1 mL
Milk	⅓ cup	75 mL
Liquid gravy browner	½ tsp.	2 mL
Extra lean ground beef	1½ lbs.	680 g

(continued on next page)

GRAVY

Can of condensed cream of mushroom and onion soup	10 oz.	284 mL
Milk	¼ cup	60 mL
Beef bouillon powder	1 tsp.	5 mL

Stir first 5 ingredients together in large bowl.

Add ground beef. Mix well. Shape into 1½ inch (3.8 cm) balls. Place in 3½ quart (3.5 L) slow cooker.

Gravy: Empty soup into medium bowl. Stir vigorously. Add milk and bouillon powder. Mix in. Pour over meatballs. Cover. Cook on Low for 8 to 9 hours or on High for 4 to 4½ hours. Makes 30 meatballs and 1⅓ cups (325 mL) gravy. Serves 6.

1 serving: 375 Calories; 20.8 g Total Fat; 683 mg Sodium; 32 g Protein; 13 g Carbohydrate; trace Dietary Fiber

---

Teriyaki Steak

Very teriyaki. Soy taste with a hint of sweetness. Serve over rice.

Boneless beef chuck (or round) steak, cut into thin strips	2 lbs.	900 g
Soy sauce	½ cup	125 mL
Beef bouillon powder	1 tbsp.	15 mL
Brown sugar, packed	1½ tbsp.	25 mL
Ground ginger	¼ tsp.	1 mL
Garlic powder	¼ tsp.	1 mL
Onion powder	¼ tsp.	1 mL
Water	½ cup	125 mL
Cornstarch (optional)	2 tbsp.	30 mL
Water (optional)	3 tbsp.	50 mL

Arrange beef strips in 3½ quart (3.5 L) slow cooker.

Stir next 7 ingredients in small bowl. Pour over beef. Stir. Cover. Cook on Low for 6 to 7 hours or on High for 3 to 3½ hours.

To thicken, combine cornstarch and second amount of water in small dish. Turn slow cooker to High. Stir in cornstarch mixture. Cook until clear and slightly thickened. Makes 4 cups (1 L). Serves 8.

1 serving: 158 Calories; 2.5 g Total Fat; 1375 mg Sodium; 28 g Protein; 5 g Carbohydrate; trace Dietary Fiber

Pictured on page 126.

Beef Bourguignon

*Serve over broad noodles or mashed potatoes — either way,
your guests will be impressed.*

Baby carrots	1 lb.	454 g
Small onions, peeled and quartered	4	4
Bacon slices, cut crosswise into ½ inch (12 mm) pieces	6	6
Beef top round steak, trimmed and cubed	1½ lbs.	680 g
Garlic powder	½ tsp.	2 mL
Freshly ground pepper, sprinkle		
Fresh small button mushrooms	3 cups	750 mL
Water	¾ cup	175 mL
Beef bouillon powder	4 tsp.	20 mL
Dry (or alcohol-free) red wine	½ cup	125 mL
Dried thyme	¼ tsp.	1 mL
Bay leaves	2	2
Cornstarch	1 tbsp.	15 mL
Cold water	2 tbsp.	30 mL

Place carrots, then onions in bottom of 6½ quart (6.5 L) slow cooker.

Fry bacon in large frying pan until crisp and browned. Remove with slotted spoon to paper towels. Drain fat, leaving 1 tbsp. (15 mL) in pan. Add steak cubes to hot fat. Sprinkle with garlic powder and pepper. Turn pieces several times until well browned. Add to slow cooker.

Quickly sauté mushrooms in same pan until lightly browned. Add to slow cooker.

Add water, bouillon powder, wine, thyme and bay leaves to same frying pan. Heat to boiling, scraping up any brown bits from pan. Pour into slow cooker. Cover. Cook on Low for 7 to 8 hours or on High for 3½ to 4 hours until beef is very tender and carrots are cooked.

Combine cornstarch and water in small dish. Stir into stew. Cook on High for about 10 minutes until slightly thickened and clear. Discard bay leaves. Makes 9 cups (2.25 L).

1 cup (250 mL): 232 Calories; 10.7 g Total Fat; 437 mg Sodium; 20 g Protein; 11 g Carbohydrate; 2 g Dietary Fiber

Pictured on page 126.

Chicken And Stuffing Meal

A great meal to come home to.

Baby carrots, sliced lengthwise	24	24
Tiny whole potatoes	24	24
Boneless, skinless chicken breast halves (about 6), cut bite size	1½ lbs.	680 g
Can of condensed cream of chicken soup	10 oz.	284 mL
Frozen peas	2 cups	500 mL
Hot water	½ cup	125 mL
Hard margarine (or butter)	2 tbsp.	30 mL
Herb stuffing mix (such as Stove Top Stuffing)	6¼ oz.	177 g

Place carrots, then potatoes in bottom of 3½ quart (3.5 L) slow cooker. Layer chicken over potatoes.

Whisk soup in small bowl. Add peas to soup. Stir gently. Spoon over chicken.

Stir hot water and margarine in medium bowl to melt margarine. Add stuffing breadcrumbs and flavoring packet. Stir. Spoon over chicken mixture. Cover. Cook on Low for 8 to 9 hours or on High for 4 to 4½ hours. Serves 6.

1 serving: 466 Calories; 9.8 g Total Fat; 991 mg Sodium; 37 g Protein; 57 g Carbohydrate; 6 g Dietary Fiber

 When cooking stews, chilies or soups in a slow cooker, allow at least 2 inches (5 cm) at the top of the crock for simmering space.

Chicken And Rice Bake

Vegetables are a bit saucy. Chicken is terrific.

Can of condensed cream of chicken soup	10 oz.	284 mL
Sliced fresh mushrooms	½ cup	125 mL
Long grain white rice	1¼ cups	300 mL
Water	2 cups	500 mL
Boneless, skinless chicken breast halves (about 1 lb., 454 g)	4	4
Dry onion soup mix (stir before measuring)	1 tbsp.	15 mL
Frozen peas	1 cup	250 mL

Stir chicken soup, mushrooms, rice and water together in 3½ quart (3.5 L) slow cooker.

Lay chicken over top. Sprinkle with dry onion soup. Scatter peas over top. Cover. Cook on Low for 7 to 8 hours or on High for 3½ to 4 hours. Serves 4.

1 serving: 461 Calories; 6.6 g Total Fat; 1048 mg Sodium; 35 g Protein; 62 g Carbohydrate; 3 g Dietary Fiber

Chicken Parmigiana

This simple dish uses commercial sauce and deserves good ratings.

Medium eggplant, with peel, sliced ¾ inch (2 cm) thick	1	1
Boneless, skinless chicken breast halves (about 1½ lbs., 680 g)	6	6
Jar of pizza sauce	14 oz.	398 mL
Salt	1 tsp.	5 mL
Pepper	¼ tsp.	1 mL
Grated part-skim mozzarella cheese	1½ cups	375 mL
Grated Parmesan cheese	1 tbsp.	15 mL

(continued on next page)

Arrange eggplant slices in bottom of 6½ quart (6.5 L) slow cooker. Lay chicken breasts over top.

Stir pizza sauce, salt and pepper together in small bowl. Pour over chicken. Cover. Cook on Low for 6 to 7 hours or on High for 3 to 3½ hours.

Sprinkle with mozzarella cheese, then Parmesan cheese. Cover. Cook on High for about 5 minutes until cheese is melted. Serves 6.

1 serving: 260 Calories; 7.2 g Total Fat; 1065 mg Sodium; 36 g Protein; 13 g Carbohydrate; 4 g Dietary Fiber

Pictured on page 126.

Lemon Cheese

Fill tart shells or spread on toast. Do not extend cooking time or cook on High.

Margarine (or butter)	⅓ cup	75 mL
Medium lemons	3	3
Fine (berry) sugar	1½ cups	375 mL
Large eggs, fork-beaten	3	3

Melt margarine in medium saucepan. Squeeze juice from lemons into small bowl. Add to margarine. Grate enough peel for 1 tbsp. (15 mL). Add to margarine mixture. Stir in sugar. Discard lemons. Stir juice mixture until sugar is dissolved. Cool to room temperature. Pour into 4 cup (1 L) glass bowl.

Stir in eggs. Cover tightly with foil. Set into bottom of 6½ quart (6.5 L) slow cooker. Pour boiling water around bowl until level is half way up sides of bowl. Cover. Cook on Low for 3 hours. Mixture will thicken as it cools. Keep chilled for up to 2 weeks. Do not freeze. Makes 2⅓ cups (575 mL).

2 tbsp. (30 mL): 109 Calories; 4.1 g Total Fat; 44 mg Sodium; 1 g Protein; 18 g Carbohydrate; trace Dietary Fiber

Berry Rhubarb Dumpling Dessert

Serve warm with frozen yogurt or fresh cream. Reserve some berries for garnish.

Chopped fresh rhubarb	2 cups	500 mL
Fresh strawberries (or frozen, thawed, with juice), sliced	1⅓ cups	325 mL
Fresh blueberries (or frozen, thawed, with juice)	1⅓ cups	325 mL
Fresh raspberries (or frozen, thawed, with juice)	1⅓ cups	325 mL
Granulated sugar	¾ cup	175 mL
Cornstarch	4 tsp.	20 mL
DUMPLINGS		
All-purpose flour	1½ cups	375 mL
Baking powder	1 tbsp.	15 mL
Granulated sugar	2 tbsp.	30 mL
Salt	½ tsp.	2 mL
Hard margarine (or butter), melted	¼ cup	60 mL
Milk	⅔ cup	150 mL
Vanilla	1 tsp.	5 mL

Layer fruit in 3½ quart (3.5 L) slow cooker in order given.

Combine sugar and cornstarch in small bowl. Sprinkle over fruit. Do not stir. Cover. Cook on High for 1½ hours. Stir.

Dumplings: Combine first 4 ingredients in medium bowl.

Combine margarine, milk and vanilla in small bowl. Stir all at once into dry ingredients to make a soft sticky dough. Spoon in 8 dollops over surface of fruit. Cover. Cook on High for about 30 minutes until dumplings are firm and risen. Makes 4 cups (1 L) fruit after cooking and 8 dumplings. Serves 8.

1 serving: 285 Calories; 6.5 g Total Fat; 256 mg Sodium; 4 g Protein; 54 g Carbohydrate; 4 g Dietary Fiber

Pictured on front cover.

Paré Pointer

He never hunted bear but went fishing in his shorts.

Slow Cooker

Toaster Oven

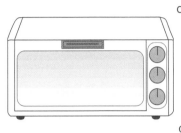

A toaster oven with broil, bake and toast controls was used to test the recipes in this section. Read your owner's manual to learn your model's features and limitations. Toaster ovens are very energy efficient and cost-effective for heating or baking smaller quantities of food.

Stuffed Mushrooms

Zippy little morsels. Very good with hot sauce.

Can of crabmeat, drained, cartilage removed, flaked	4¼ oz.	120 g
Salad dressing (or mayonnaise)	1 tbsp.	15 mL
Lemon juice	1¼ tsp.	6 mL
Onion powder	⅛ tsp.	0.5 mL
Garlic powder	⅛ tsp.	0.5 mL
Chopped chives	2 tsp.	10 mL
Pepper (optional)	⅛ tsp.	0.5 mL
Hot pepper sauce (optional)	⅛ tsp.	0.5 mL
Medium mushrooms, stems removed	16	16
Grated fresh Parmesan cheese	4 tsp.	20 mL

Mix first 8 ingredients well in small bowl.

Stuff mushroom caps. Discard stems or reserve for another use. Sprinkle with cheese. Arrange on ungreased toaster oven pan. Chill until needed. Preheat toaster oven to 400°F (205°C). Bake mushrooms for 10 to 12 minutes until hot. Makes 16.

1 stuffed mushroom: 18 Calories; 1 g Total Fat; 64 mg Sodium; 2 g Protein; 1 g Carbohydrate; trace Dietary Fiber

Pictured on page 143.

Baked Brie

Dark cranberry over white brie makes a nice color contrast and flavor combination. Serve with your favorite crackers.

Round of brie	8 oz.	225 g
Ground cinnamon	⅛ tsp.	0.5 mL
Whole cranberry sauce	½ cup	125 mL

Place brie in ungreased 6 inch (15 cm) ovenproof serving dish. Bake in 350°F (175°C) toaster oven for 10 to 12 minutes until cheese feels soft when sides are pressed.

Mix cinnamon and cranberry sauce in small bowl. Spoon over top of brie. Bake for about 5 minutes to warm cranberry sauce. Makes ⅔ cup (150 mL) sauce plus brie. Serves 10.

1 serving: 97 Calories; 6.3 g Total Fat; 146 mg Sodium; 5 g Protein; 6 g Carbohydrate; trace Dietary Fiber

Pictured on page 143.

Baked Cheese

This can be served as an appetizer or as a lunch dish. Serve with plenty of nacho chips or spread on firm crackers.

Grated sharp Cheddar cheese	2 cups	500 mL
All-purpose flour	1 tbsp.	15 mL
Salsa	¾ cup	175 mL
All-purpose flour	1 tbsp.	15 mL
Grated Monterey Jack cheese	2 cups	500 mL

Toss first amount of flour and Cheddar cheese together. Place in bottom of 9 inch (22 cm) pie plate.

Spread salsa over top.

Toss second amount of flour with Monterey Jack cheese. Place over salsa. Bake in 325°F (160°C) toaster oven for 25 minutes. Makes about 2 cups (500 mL).

1 tbsp. (15 mL): 64 Calories; 4.7 g Total Fat; 178 mg Sodium; 4 g Protein; 1 g Carbohydrate; trace Dietary Fiber

Toaster Oven

Poutine

Perfect for one serving.

Frozen french-fried potatoes (about 2 cups, 500 mL)	6 oz.	170 g
Grated part-skim mozzarella cheese	⅓ cup	75 mL
Gravy mix, prepared according to directions	⅓-½ cup	75-125 mL

Spread potatoes on greased toaster oven pan. Bake in 400°F (205°C) toaster oven for about 15 minutes until crisp and browned.

Sprinkle with mozzarella cheese. Pour hot gravy over cheese. Serves 1.

1 serving: 511 Calories; 22 g Total Fat; 741 mg Sodium; 17 g Protein; 64 g Carbohydrate; 5 g Dietary Fiber

Pictured on page 144.

Tuna Snack Buns

Tangy and slightly sweet topping on a crispy bun.

Can of tuna, drained	6½ oz.	184 g
Sweet pickle relish	2 tbsp.	30 mL
Light salad dressing (or mayonnaise)	2 tbsp.	30 mL
Hamburger buns, split (butter optional)	3	3
Light salad dressing (or mayonnaise)	¼ cup	60 mL
Grated sharp Cheddar cheese	¼ cup	60 mL

Mix tuna, relish and first amount of salad dressing in small bowl.

Divide and spread on bun halves.

Mix second amount of salad dressing and cheese in small bowl. Spread on tuna mixture. Arrange on ungreased toaster oven pan. Broil in toaster oven about 4 inches from heat for about 8 minutes until buns are crisp and cheese is melted. Makes 6.

1 tuna bun: 174 Calories; 7.6 g Total Fat; 396 mg Sodium; 11 g Protein; 15 g Carbohydrate; 1 g Dietary Fiber

WIENER SNACK BUNS: Spread buns thinly with mustard and 1 tsp. (5 mL) relish per bun. Cover with wiener slices. Spread salad dressing mixture on wieners. Broil.

Ham And Cheese Roll-ups

These golden crispy sandwiches have a pinwheel look when sliced as appetizers.

Can of ham flakes	6½ oz.	184 g
Light cream cheese, softened	4 oz.	125 g
Ketchup	1 tbsp.	15 mL
Sweet pickle relish	1 tbsp.	15 mL
White (or whole wheat) bread slices, crusts removed	10	10
Hard margarine (or butter), melted	2 tbsp.	30 mL

Mash first 4 ingredients together well in small bowl. Makes 1⅓ cups (325 mL) filling.

Roll bread slices quite thin. Spread each slice with 1 rounded tbsp. (15 mL) ham mixture. Roll up jelly-roll style.

Brush each roll on all sides with melted margarine. Arrange on ungreased toaster oven pan, seam side down. Bake in 400°F (205°C) toaster oven for about 2 minutes until browned. Cut each roll into 3 pieces. Makes 30 bite-size appetizers.

1 appetizer: 52 Calories; 2.8 g Total Fat; 180 mg Sodium; 2 g Protein; 5 g Carbohydrate; trace Dietary Fiber

1. Oriental Snack Mix, page 123
   (Slow Cooker)
2. Seafood Canapés, page 145
   (Toaster Oven)
3. Baked Brie, page 140
   (Toaster Oven)
4. Stuffed Mushrooms, page 139
   (Toaster Oven)

Props Courtesy Of: The Bay

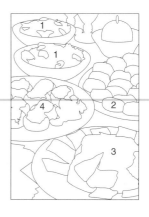

Toaster Oven

Seafood Canapés

For curry lovers. Easy to use less curry if desired.
Good little morsels. Unused topping can be frozen.

Light mayonnaise (not salad dressing)	¾ cup	175 mL
Curry powder	¾ tsp.	175 mL
Can of crabmeat, drained, cartilage removed, flaked	4¼ oz.	120 g
Grated light sharp Cheddar cheese	½ cup	125 mL
White bread slices	12	12

Mix mayonnaise, curry powder, crabmeat and cheese in medium bowl. Makes 1⅓ cups (325 mL) spread.

Cut 2 rounds, about 2 inches (5 cm) across, from each bread slice. Arrange on ungreased toaster oven pan. Toast 1 side of each round. Spread each untoasted side with scant 1 tbsp. (15 mL) crab mixture. Broil in toaster oven until browned. Makes 24.

1 canapé: 65 Calories; 3.3 g Total Fat; 156 mg Sodium; 2 g Protein; 6 g Carbohydrate; trace Dietary Fiber

Pictured on page 143.

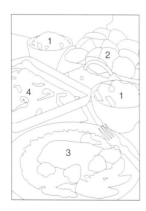

1. Poutine, page 141 **(Toaster Oven)**
2. Lasting Cereal Muffins, page 147 **(Toaster Oven)**
3. Chicken With Broccoli, page 146 **(Toaster Oven)**
4. Crescent Pizza, page 150 **(Toaster Oven)**

Props Courtesy Of: Hamilton Beach
Zenari's

Crescent Pizza

Lean ground beef can be substituted for chicken if desired.
Looks great! Tastes great!

Tube of refrigerator crescent-style rolls (8 rolls per tube)	1	1
Lean ground chicken	6 oz.	170 g
Thinly sliced onion rings	¼ cup	60 mL
White vinegar	1 tbsp.	15 mL
Chili powder	1 tsp.	5 mL
Dried whole oregano	¼ tsp.	1 mL
Garlic powder	⅛ tsp.	0.5 mL
Salt	¼ tsp.	1 mL
Cooking oil	1 tsp.	5 mL
Thinly sliced onion	¼ cup	60 mL
Small green pepper, slivered	½	½
Small red pepper, slivered	½	½
Chili sauce (or ketchup)	2 tbsp.	30 mL
Grated part-skim mozzarella cheese	1 cup	250 mL

Press dough in bottom and ½ inch (12 mm) up sides of greased toaster oven pan.

Mix next 7 ingredients well in medium bowl.

Scramble-fry chicken mixture in hot cooking oil in frying pan until no pink remains. Remove to plate.

Add onion and peppers to frying pan. Sauté until tender-crisp.

Spread chili sauce on dough. Layer chicken mixture, onion and peppers over chili sauce. Sprinkle with mozzarella cheese. Bake in 425°F (220°C) toaster oven for 12 to 15 minutes until edges are browned. Cuts into 6 squares.

1 square: 232 Calories; 10.9 g Total Fat; 688 mg Sodium; 14 g Protein; 19 g Carbohydrate; 1 g Dietary Fiber

Pictured on page 144.

Lasting Cereal Muffins

A bit different than the usual bran muffin. A welcome snack any time of day.

Boiling water	½ cup	125 mL
Wheat and barley cereal (such as Grape Nuts)	1½ cups	375 mL
Hard margarine (or butter), softened	¼ cup	60 mL
Brown sugar, packed	⅔ cup	150 mL
Large egg	1	1
Buttermilk (or reconstituted from powder)	1 cup	250 mL
Fancy (mild) molasses	1 tbsp.	15 mL
Chopped dates (or raisins)	1 cup	250 mL
All-purpose flour	¾ cup	175 mL
Whole wheat flour	⅔ cup	150 mL
Baking soda	1¼ tsp.	6 mL
Baking powder	1 tsp.	5 mL
Salt	¼ tsp.	1 mL

Pour boiling water over cereal in medium bowl. Stir. Let stand for 10 minutes.

Cream margarine and brown sugar in large bowl. Beat in egg. Add buttermilk, molasses and dates. Add cereal. Stir.

Add both flours, baking soda, baking powder and salt. Stir to moisten. Store in refrigerator in covered plastic container. When ready to bake, fill 6 greased muffin cups almost full. Bake in 400°F (205°C) toaster oven for 18 minutes. Repeat with remaining batter. Makes 18 muffins.

1 muffin: 166 Calories; 3.4 g Total Fat; 250 mg Sodium; 4 g Protein; 32 g Carbohydrate; 3 g Dietary Fiber

Pictured on page 144.

 Reheating foil-wrapped food in a toaster oven will be faster if you open the foil slightly and will prevent steam from building up.

French Bread Pizza

Good tomato and pepperoni flavor. A great snack.

Pizza sauce	1 cup	250 mL
French loaf, split in half horizontally	1	1
Sliced pepperoni	½ cup	125 mL
Grated part-skim mozzarella cheese	1 cup	250 mL

Spread ½ of pizza sauce on each loaf layer. Cut loaf layers in half crosswise if necessary to fit into toaster oven. Divide pepperoni over top. Sprinkle with cheese. Place on ungreased toaster oven pan. Bake in 375°F (190°C) toaster oven for 12 minutes until cheese is melted. Cut each section into thirds, for a total of 12 slices.

1 slice: 175 Calories; 5.6 g Total Fat; 510 mg Sodium; 7 g Protein; 23 g Carbohydrate; 1 g Dietary Fiber

Variation: Split 3 submarine buns in half horizontally. Divide and layer pizza sauce, pepperoni and cheese over each half. Bake as above.

Pictured on front cover.

Bonnie Bluefish

With a hint of lemon and onion. Good combo.

Package of bluefish, thawed and separated into 4 pieces	14 oz.	400 g
Light sour cream	½ cup	125 mL
Lemon juice	1 tsp.	5 mL
Minced onion flakes	1½ tsp.	7 mL
Garlic salt	¼ tsp.	1 mL
Paprika	¼ tsp.	1 mL
Parsley flakes	¼ tsp.	1 mL

Arrange bluefish in single layer in greased toaster oven pan.

Stir sour cream and lemon juice together in small bowl. Add onion flakes, garlic salt, paprika and parsley flakes. Stir. Spoon over fish. Bake in 375°F (190°C) toaster oven for 20 minutes until fish flakes when tested with fork. Serves 4.

1 serving: 155 Calories; 6.4 g Total Fat; 162 mg Sodium; 21 g Protein; 2 g Carbohydrate; trace Dietary Fiber

Chicken With Broccoli

Broccoli stays crisp and green, making a nice color contrast to the cheese sauce.
Serve over rice.

Boneless, skinless chicken breast halves	4	4
(about 1 lb., 454 g)		
Seasoned salt	½ tsp.	2 mL
Pepper	¼ tsp.	1 mL
Milk	1 cup	250 mL
All-purpose flour	2 tbsp.	30 mL
Grated light sharp Cheddar cheese	1 cup	250 mL
Chopped fresh broccoli	3 cups	750 mL

Arrange chicken in greased toaster oven pan. Sprinkle both sides with seasoned salt and pepper. Broil each side for about 5 minutes until browned.

Gradually whisk milk into flour in small saucepan until smooth. Heat, stirring until boiling and thickened. Stir in cheese.

Arrange broccoli around chicken. Cover with cheese sauce. Cover pan with foil. Bake in 350°F (175°C) toaster oven for 40 minutes. Remove foil. Broil if desired to brown top. Serves 4.

1 serving: 277 Calories; 8.4 g Total Fat; 486 mg Sodium; 38 g Protein; 11 g Carbohydrate;
2 g Dietary Fiber

Pictured on page 144.

Paré Pointer

When the leopard finished his meal,
he said it really hit the spots.

Measurement Tables

Throughout this book measurements are given in Conventional and Metric measure. To compensate for differences between the two measurements due to rounding, a full metric measure is not always used. The cup used is the standard 8 fluid ounce. Temperature is given in degrees Fahrenheit and Celsius. Baking pan measurements are in inches and centimetres as well as quarts and litres. An exact metric conversion is given below as well as the working equivalent (Standard Measure).

Spoons

Conventional Measure	Metric Exact Conversion Millilitre (mL)	Metric Standard Measure Millilitre (mL)
1/8 teaspoon (tsp.)	0.6 mL	0.5 mL
1/4 teaspoon (tsp.)	1.2 mL	1 mL
1/2 teaspoon (tsp.)	2.4 mL	2 mL
1 teaspoon (tsp.)	4.7 mL	5 mL
2 teaspoons (tsp.)	9.4 mL	10 mL
1 tablespoon (tbsp.)	14.2 mL	15 mL

Cups

Conventional Measure	Metric Exact Conversion Millilitre (mL)	Metric Standard Measure Millilitre (mL)
1/4 cup (4 tbsp.)	56.8 mL	60 mL
1/3 cup (5 1/3 tbsp.)	75.6 mL	75 mL
1/2 cup (8 tbsp.)	113.7 mL	125 mL
2/3 cup (10 2/3 tbsp.)	151.2 mL	150 mL
3/4 cup (12 tbsp.)	170.5 mL	175 mL
1 cup (16 tbsp.)	227.3 mL	250 mL
4 1/2 cups	1022.9 mL	1000 mL (1 L)

Oven Temperatures

Fahrenheit (°F)	Celsius (°C)
175°	80°
200°	95°
225°	110°
250°	120°
275°	140°
300°	150°
325°	160°
350°	175°
375°	190°
400°	205°
425°	220°
450°	230°
475°	240°
500°	260°

Dry Measurements

Conventional Measure Ounces (oz.)	Metric Exact Conversion Grams (g)	Metric Standard Measure Grams (g)
1 oz.	28.3 g	28 g
2 oz.	56.7 g	57 g
3 oz.	85.0 g	85 g
4 oz.	113.4 g	125 g
5 oz.	141.7 g	140 g
6 oz.	170.1 g	170 g
7 oz.	198.4 g	200 g
8 oz.	226.8 g	250 g
16 oz.	453.6 g	500 g
32 oz.	907.2 g	1000 g (1 kg)

Pans

Conventional Inches	Metric Centimetres
8x8 inch	20x20 cm
9x9 inch	22x22 cm
9x13 inch	22x33 cm
10x15 inch	25x38 cm
11x17 inch	28x43 cm
8x2 inch round	20x5 cm
9x2 inch round	22x5 cm
10x4 1/2 inch tube	25x11 cm
8x4x3 inch loaf	20x10x7.5 cm
9x5x3 inch loaf	22x12.5x7.5 cm

Casseroles

CANADA & BRITAIN		UNITED STATES	
Standard Size Casserole	Exact Metric Measure	Standard Size Casserole	Exact Metric Measure
1 qt. (5 cups)	1.13 L	1 qt. (5 cups)	900 mL
1 1/2 qts. (7 1/2 cups)	1.69 L	1 1/2 qts. (7 1/2 cups)	1.35 L
2 qts. (10 cups)	2.25 L	2 qts. (10 cups)	1.8 L
2 1/2 qts. (12 1/2 cups)	2.81 L	2 1/2 qts. (12 1/2 cups)	2.25 L
3 qts. (15 cups)	3.38 L	3 qts. (15 cups)	2.7 L
4 qts. (20 cups)	4.5 L	4 qts. (20 cups)	3.6 L
5 qts. (25 cups)	5.63 L	5 qts. (25 cups)	4.5 L

Index

B – Blender	J – Juicer
BM – Bread Machine	PC – Pressure Cooker
EF – Electric Frying Pan	SM – Sandwich Maker
FP – Food Processor	SC – Slow Cooker
HB – Hand Blender	TO – Toaster Oven

Ale, Fizzy (J) 82
Appetizers
  Baked Brie (TO) 140
  Baked Cheese (TO) 140
  Cheese Bread (BM) 32
  Ham And Cheese Roll-Ups (TO) 142
  Oriental Snack Mix (SC) 123
  Seafood Canapés (TO) 145
  Stuffed Mushrooms (TO) 139
Apple Pork Chops (PC) 103
Apples, Spicy Stuffed (PC) 110
Apricot Chicken (EF) 34

Baby Food
  Broccoli Purée (FP) 66
  Puréed Carrots (FP) 65
  Puréed Chicken Dinner (FP) 64
  Squash Purée (FP) 66
  Sweet Potato Purée (FP) 65
Baked Brie (TO) 140
Baked Cheese (TO) 140
Banana
  Choco Banana Shake (B) 14
  Peach Banana Frost (B) 13
  Peanut Banana Shake (B) 14
  Virgin Banana Daiquiri (B) 16
Banana Daiquiri (B) 16
Banana Orange Milk Shake (B) 14
Banana Toasties (SM) 120
Barley, Curried Beef And (EF) 33
Basil Pesto (HB) 68
Béarnaise Sauce (B) 9
Beef
  Chili Snacks (SM) 115
  Chinese Pepper Steak (SC) 130
  Curried (SC) .132
  Curried Beef And Barley (EF) 33
  Meatballs In Gravy (SC) 132
  Spaghetti Sauce And Meatballs (SC) . .128
  Steak Bake (SC) 131
  Stewed Beef And Dumplings (PC) 96
  Teriyaki Steak (SC) 133
  Vegetable Beef Soup (PC) 94
Beef Bourguignon (SC) 134
Beef Stew (PC) .95
Beefy Bun Topping (SC) 129
Beet Bonanza (J) 84
Berry Cheesy Sweet (SM) 121
Berry Cooler (B) 11
Berry Diet Shake (HB) 67
Berry Drink Concentrate (J) 83
Berry Juice, Very (J) 80
Berry Syrup, Very (J) 88
Berry Rhubarb Dumpling Dessert (SC) . .138
Beverages
  Banana Daiquiri (B) 16
  Banana Orange Milk Shake (B) 14

Beet Bonanza (J) 84
Berry Cooler (B) 11
Berry Diet Shake (HB) 67
Berry Drink Concentrate (J) 83
Choco Banana Shake (B) 14
Egg Nog (B) 15
Fizzy Ale (J) 82
Frosty Peach (B) 13
Frozen Strawberry Daiquiri (B) 19
Fruit Punch (J) 80
Grape Chill (B) 13
Green Zinger (J) 84
Lemon Slush (B) 12
Margarita Slush (B) 20
Melon Drink (J) 81
Orange Freeze (B) 12
Orange Milk Froth (B) 20
Orange Vegetable Brew (J) 81
Orchard Juice (J) 79
Peach Banana Frost (B) 13
Peanut Banana Shake (B) 14
Piña Colada Shake (B) 14
Pineapple Peach Shake (B) 14
Pineapple Shake (B) 14
Pink Margarita Slush (B) 20
Spicy Veggie Brew (J) 85
Straw-Barb Juice (J) 83
Strawberry Milk Shake (B) 15
Tropical Breeze (J) 82
Very Berry Juice (J) 80
Virgin Banana Daiquiri (B) 16
Virgin Strawberry Daiquiri (B) 19
Winter Veggies Drink (J) 85
Biscuit Pizza Crust (FP) 55
Black Bean Soup (HB) 74
Blender Hollandaise Sauce (B) 9
Blue Cheese Dressing (B) 22
Blue Cheese Mayo, Mock (B) 23
Bluefish, Bonnie (TO) 148
Bonnie Bluefish (TO) 148
Boston Brown Bread (SC) 122
Bourguignon, Beef (SC) 134
Bread Pudding (PC) 106
Breads & Quickbreads
  Biscuit Pizza Crust (FP) 55
  Boston Brown (SC) 122
  Cheese (BM) .32
  Corn (BM) 27
  Cottage Dill (BM) 30
  Cracked Wheat (BM) 28
  Dill (BM) 30
  Herb (BM) 32
  Honey Wheat (BM) 29
  Lasting Cereal Muffins (TO) 147
  Maple Wheat Bread (BM) 25
  Oatmeal (BM) 26
  Orange Poppy Seed (BM) 29

Panettone (BM) 24
Parmesan (BM) 27
Pizza Crust (FP) 56
Pizza Wheat Crust (FP) 57
Potato (BM) 30
Pumpernickel (BM) 25
Sally Lunn (BM) 31
Shredded Wheat (BM) 26
Swedish Rye (BM) 31
Tropical Loaf (J) 91
Whole Wheat (BM) 28
Whole Wheat Twists (FP) 58
Brie, Baked (TO) 140
Broccoli, Chicken With (TO) 149
Broccoli Purée (FP) 66
Brown Bread, Boston (SC) 122
Buns, Tuna Snack (TO) 141
Butter Icing (HB) 77

Cacciatore, Chicken (PC) 98
Caesar Salad Dressing (B) 21
Cakes
    Caramel Pecan Cheesecake (PC) 111
    Carrot (J)......................87
    Chocolate (HB) 76
    Chocolate Pudding (PC) 109
    Dark Fruitcake (PC) 113
    White (FP).....................63
    White Fruitcake (PC) 112
Canapés, Seafood (TO) 145
Cantonese, Shrimp (EF) 45
Caramel Pecan Cheesecake (PC) 111
Carrot Cake (J)...................87
Carrots, Puréed (FP) 65
Cereal Muffins, Lasting (TO) 147
Cheese, Baked (TO) 175
Cheese Bread (BM) 32
Cheese Gnocchi (FP) 60
Cheese, Lemon (SC) 140
Cheese Roll-Ups, Ham And (TO) 142
Cheesecake, Caramel Pecan (PC) 111
Chicken
    Apricot (EF) 34
    Crescent Pizza (TO) 146
    Pacific (PC) 99
    Pineapple (EF) 40
    Puréed Chicken Dinner (FP) 64
    Sweet And Sour (PC) 97
Chicken And Rice Bake (SC) 136
Chicken And Stuffing Meal (SC) 135
Chicken Cacciatore (PC) 98
Chicken Dinner, Puréed (FP) 64
Chicken Fried Rice (EF) 41
Chicken Mornay (EF) 39
Chicken Parmigiana (SC) 136
Chicken Patties (EF) 42
Chicken Peking (EF) 37
Chicken Stew (EF) 38
Chicken With Broccoli (TO) 149
Chili Snacks (SM) 115
Chinese Pepper Steak (SC) 130
Choco Banana Shake (B) 14
Chocolate Cake (HB) 76
Chocolate Icing (HB) 77
Chocolate Pudding Cake (PC) 109

Chops, Apple Pork (PC) 103
Chops, Cranberry-Glazed (EF) 47
Chops Supreme, Pork (PC) 102
Chowder, Seafood (PC) 93
Coffee Icing (HB) 77
Coleslaw (FP).....................52
Concentrate, Berry Drink (J) 83
Cooler, Berry (B) 11
Cottage Dill Bread (BM) 30
Corn Bread (BM) 27
Corn Fritters (SM) 117
Crabby Packets (SM) 116
Cracked Wheat Bread (BM) 28
Cranberry-Glazed Chops (EF) 47
Cream Cheese Icing (J) 87
Crêpes (B)........................8
Crescent Pizza (TO) 146
Crusts
    Biscuit Pizza (FP) 55
    Pizza (FP) 56
    Pizza Wheat (FP) 57
    Thin Pizza (FP) 56
Curried Beef (SC) 132
Curried Beef And Barley (EF) 33
Curry, Lamb (PC) 100

Daiquiris
    Banana (B) 16
    Frozen Strawberry (B) 19
    Virgin Banana (B) 16
    Virgin Strawberry (B) 19
Dark Fruitcake (PC)...............113
Date Pie (HB) 78
Desserts
    Banana Toasties (SM) 120
    Berry Cheesy Sweet (SM) 121
    Berry Rhubarb Dumpling(SC) 138
    Bread Pudding (PC) 106
    Butter Icing (HB) 77
    Caramel Pecan Cheesecake (PC) 111
    Carrot Cake (J) 87
    Chocolate Cake (HB) 76
    Chocolate Icing (HB) 77
    Chocolate Pudding Cake (PC) 109
    Coffee Icing (HB) 77
    Cream Cheese Icing (J) 87
    Crêpes (B)......................8
    Dark Fruit Cake (PC) 113
    Date Pie (HB) 78
    Holiday Pudding (PC) 105
    Mince Pie Singles (SM) 118
    Raisin Pies (SM) 119
    Shortbread (FP) 62
    S'more Toasts (SM) 120
    Spicy Stuffed Apples (PC) 110
    Very Berry Syrup (J) 88
    White Cake (FP) 63
    White Fruitcake (PC) 112
Diet Shake, Berry (HB) 67
Dill Bread (BM) 30
Dill Bread, Cottage (BM) 30
Dips & Spreads
    Herbed Feta Dip (HB) 73
    Lemon Cheese (SC) 137
    Mock Blue Cheese Mayo (B) 23

Quick Salsa (FP) 49
Red Pepper Dip (HB) 69
Shrimp Spread (HB) 69
Sundried Tomato Pesto Spread (B) 10
Vegetable Topper (B) 11
Dressed Red Potatoes (SC) 127
Dressings
Blue Cheese (B) 22
Caesar Salad (B) 21
French-Type (B) 22
Italian-Type (B) 21
Dumpling Dessert, Berry Rhubarb (SC) .138
Dumplings (EF) 38
Dumplings, Stewed Beef And (PC) 96

Egg Nog (B) .15

Feta Dip, Herbed (HB) 73
Fish & Seafood
Bonnie Bluefish (TO) 148
Crabby Packets (SM) 116
Hot Tuna Sandwiches (SM) 114
Poached Salmon (EF) 44
Seafood Chowder (PC) 93
Shrimp Cantonese (EF) 45
Fizzy Ale (J) .82
French Bread Pizza (TO) 148
French Onion Soup (PC) 92
French-Type Dressing (B) 22
Fried Rice, Chicken (EF) 41
Fritters, Corn (SM) 117
Frosty Peach (B) 13
Frozen Strawberry Daiquiri (B) 19
Fruitcake, Dark (PC) 113
Fruitcake, White (PC) 112
Fruit Punch (J) 80

Garden Pea Soup (HB) 74
Glazed Chops, Cranberry-(EF) 47
Glazed Ham Slice (EF) 44
Gnocchi, Cheese (FP) 60
Grape Chill (B) 13
Gravy, Meatballs In (SC) 132
Green Zinger (J) 84

Ham And Cheese Roll-Ups (TO) 142
Ham Slice, Glazed (EF) 44
Herb Bread (BM) 32
Herbed Feta Dip (HB) 73
Holiday Pudding (PC) 105
Hollandaise Sauce, Blender (B) 9
Honey Wheat Bread (BM) 29
Hot Tuna Sandwiches (SM) 114

Icing
Butter (HB) 77
Chocolate (HB) 77
Coffee (HB) 77
Cream Cheese (J) 87
Italian-Type Dressing (B) 21

Jambalaya, Pork (PC) 104

Lamb Curry (PC) 100
Lamb, Rack of (PC) 101

Lasting Cereal Muffins (TO) 147
Lemon Cheese (SC) 137
Lemon Slush (B) 12
Loaf, Tropical (J) 91
Lunch
Baked Cheese (TO) 140
Cheese Bread (BM) 32
Chili Snacks (SM) 115
Crabby Packets (SM) 116
Crescent Pizza (TO) 146
French Bread Pizza (TO) 148
Ham And Cheese Roll-Ups (TO) 142
Poutine (TO) 141
Tuna Snack Buns (TO) 141
Lunchtime Tater Cakes (SM) 116

Main Dishes
Apple Pork Chops (PC) 103
Apricot Chicken (EF) 34
Beef Bourguignon (SC) 134
Beef Stew (PC) 95
Bonnie Bluefish (TO) 148
Cheese Gnocchi (FP) 60
Chicken And Rice Bake (SC) 136
Chicken And Stuffing Meal (SC) 135
Chicken Cacciatore (PC) 98
Chicken Fried Rice (EF) 41
Chicken Mornay (EF) 39
Chicken Parmigiana (SC) 136
Chicken Patties (EF) 42
Chicken Peking (EF) 37
Chicken Stew (EF) 38
Chicken With Broccoli (TO) 149
Chinese Pepper Steak (SC) 130
Cranberry-Glazed Chops (EF) 47
Curried Beef (SC) 132
Curried Beef And Barley (EF) 33
Glazed Ham Slice (EF) 44
Lamb Curry (PC) 100
Meatballs In Gravy (SC) 132
Pacific Chicken (PC) 99
Pineapple Chicken (EF) 40
Poached Salmon (EF) 44
Pork Chops Supreme (PC) 102
Pork Jambalaya (PC) 104
Rack Of Lamb (PC) 101
Ribs Delight (PC) 102
Shrimp Cantonese (EF) 45
Spaghetti Sauce And Meatballs (SC) . .128
Steak Bake (SC) 131
Stewed Beef And Dumplings (PC) 96
Sweet And Sour Chicken (PC) 97
Sweet And Sour Ribs (EF) 46
Teriyaki Steak (SC) 133
Turkey Patties (EF) 42
Turkey Stroganoff (EF) 43
Make-Ahead Potatoes (SC) 124
Maple Wheat Bread (BM) 25
Margarita Slush (B) 20
Margarita Slush, Pink (B) 20
Mayo, Mock Blue Cheese (B) 23
Meatballs (SC) 128
Meatballs In Gravy (SC) 132
Meatballs, Spaghetti Sauce And (SC) . . .128
Melon Drink (J) 81

Mince Pie Singles (SM) 118
Milk Froth, Orange (B) 20
Milk Shakes, see Shakes
Mixed Slaw (FP) 51
Mock Blue Cheese Mayo (B) 23
Mock Sour Cream (B) 23
Monte Cristo Sandwich (SM) 118
Mornay Sauce (EF) 39
Muffins, Lasting Cereal (TO) 147
Mushrooms, Stuffed (TO) 139

Navy Bean Soup (PC) 94

Oatmeal Bread (BM) 26
Onion Soup, French (PC) 92
Orange Freeze (B) 12
Orange Milk Froth (B) 20
Orange Milk Shake, Banana (B) 14
Orange Poppy Seed Bread (BM) 29
Orange Vegetable Brew (J) 81
Orchard Juice (J) 79
Oriental Snack Mix (SC) 123

Pacific Chicken (PC) 99
Panettone (BM) 24
Parmesan Bread (BM) 27
Parmigiana, Chicken (SC) 136
Pastas
  Cheese Gnocchi (FP) 60
  Spaghetti Sandwich (SM) 115
Pastry, Pie (FP) 62
Pastry, Wheat (FP) 61
Patties, Chicken (EF) 42
Patties, Turkey (EF) 42
Pea Soup, Garden (HB) 74
Pea Soup, Split (HB) 75
Peach Banana Frost (B) 13
Peach, Frosty (B) 13
Peach Shake, Pineapple (B) 14
Peanut Banana Shake (B) 14
Peanut Sauce, Spicy (HB) 70
Pecan Cheesecake, Caramel (PC) 111
Peking, Chicken (EF) 37
Pepper Dip, Red (HB) 69
Pepper Steak, Chinese (SC) 130
Pesto
  Basil (HB) 68
  Sundried Tomato (B) 10
  Sundried Tomato Pesto Spread (B) 10
Pie, Date (HB) 78
Pie Pastry (FP) 62
Pies, Raisin (SM) 119
Piña Colada Shake (B) 14
Pineapple Chicken (EF) 40
Pineapple Peach Shake (B) 14
Pineapple Shake (B) 14
Pink Margarita Slush (B) 20
Pizzas
  Biscuit Pizza Crust (FP) 55
  Crescent (TO) 146
  French Bread (TO) 148
  Thin Pizza Crust (FP) 56
Pizza Crust (FP) 56
Pizza Wheat Crust (FP) 57
Poached Salmon (EF) 44
Poppy Seed Bread, Orange (BM) 29

Pork
  Apple Pork Chops (PC) 103
  Cranberry-Glazed Chops (EF) 47
  Glazed Ham Slice (EF) 44
  Monte Cristo Sandwich (SM) 118
  Navy Bean Soup (PC) 94
  Ribs Delight (PC) 102
  Sweet And Sour Ribs (EF) 46
Pork Chops, Apple (PC) 103
Pork Chops Supreme (PC) 102
Pork Jambalaya (PC) 104
Potato Bread (BM) 30
Potato Salad (FP) 50
Potatoes, Dressed Red (SC) 127
Potatoes, Make-Ahead (SC) 124
Potatoes, Scalloped (FP) 59
Poutine (TO) 141
Pudding, Bread (PC) 106
Pudding Cake, Chocolate (PC) 109
Pudding, Holiday (PC) 105
Pulp Soup, Vegetable (J) 86
Pumpernickel Bread (BM) 25
Punch, Fruit (J) 80
Purée
  Broccoli (FP) 66
  Squash (FP) 66
  Sweet Potato (FP) 65
Puréed Carrots (FP) 65
Puréed Chicken Dinner (FP) 64

Quick Salsa (FP) 49
Quickbreads, See Breads & Quickbreads

Rack Of Lamb (PC) 101
Raisin Pies (SM) 119
Red Pepper Dip (HB) 69
Red Potatoes, Dressed (SC) 127
Rhubarb Dumpling Dessert, Berry (SC) .138
Ribs Delight (PC) 102
Ribs, Sweet And Sour (EF) 46
Rice Bake, Chicken And (SC) 136
Rice, Chicken Fried (EF) 41
Roll-Ups, Ham And Cheese (TO) 142
Rye Bread, Swedish (BM) 31

Salads
  Coleslaw (FP) 52
  Mixed Slaw (FP) 51
  Potato (FP) 50
S'more Toasts (SM) 120
Salad Dressing, Caesar (B) 21
Salad, Potato (FP) 50
Sally Lunn (BM) 31
Salmon, Poached (EF) 44
Salsa, Quick (FP) 49
Sandwiches
  Beefy Bun Topping (SC) 129
  Chili Snacks (SM) 115
  Crabby Packets (SM) 116
  Crescent Pizza (TO) 146
  French Bread Pizza (TO) 148
  Ham And Cheese Roll-Ups (TO) 142
  Hot Tuna (SM) 114
  Monte Cristo (SM) 118
  Spaghetti (SM) 115
  Tuna Snack Buns (TO) 141

Sauces
  Béarnaise (B) .9
  Blender Hollandaise (B) 9
  Mornay (EF) 39
  Spaghetti (SC) 128
  Spicy Peanut (HB) 70
  Tartar (FP) 48
Sauce And Meatballs, Spaghetti (SC) . . .128
Scalloped Potatoes (FP) 59
Seafood Canapés (TO) 145
Seafood Chowder (PC) 93
Shakes
  Banana Orange Milk (B) 14
  Berry Diet (HB) 67
  Choco Banana (B) 14
  Orange Milk Froth (B) 20
  Peanut Banana (B) 14
  Piña Colada (B) 14
  Pineapple (B) .14
  Pineapple Peach (B) 14
  Strawberry Milk (B) 15
Shortbread (FP) 62
Shredded Wheat Bread (BM) 26
Shrimp Cantonese (EF) 45
Shrimp Spread (HB) 69
Side Dishes
  Cheese Gnocchi (FP) 60
  Chicken Fried Rice (EF) 41
  Dressed Red Potatoes (SC) 127
  Make-Ahead Potatoes (SC) 124
  Scalloped Potatoes (FP) 59
Slaw, Mixed (FP) 51
Slushes
  Banana Daiquiri (B) 16
  Frosty Peach (B) 13
  Frozen Strawberry Daiquiri (B) 19
  Lemon (B) 12
  Margarita (B) .20
  Peach Banana Frost (B) 13
  Pink Margarita (B) 20
  Virgin Banana Daiquiri (B) 16
  Virgin Strawberry Daiquiri (B) 19
Snack Buns, Tuna (TO) 141
Snack Mix, Oriental (SC) 123
Snacks, Chili (SM) 115
Soups
  Black Bean (HB) 74
  French Onion (PC) 92
  Garden Pea (HB) 74
  Navy Bean (PC) 94
  Seafood Chowder (PC) 93
  Split Pea (HB) 75
  Vegetable Beef (PC) 94
  Vegetable Pulp (J) 86
Sour Cream, Mock (B) 23
Spaghetti Sandwich (SM) 115
Spaghetti Sauce And Meatballs (SC) . . .128
Spicy Peanut Sauce (HB) 70
Spicy Stuffed Apples (PC) 110
Spicy Veggie Brew (J) 85
Split Pea Soup (HB) 75
Spreads, See Dips & Spreads
Squash Purée (FP) 66
Steak Bake (SC) 131
Steak, Chinese Pepper (SC) 130

Steak, Teriyaki (SC) 133
Stew, Beef (PC) 95
Stew, Chicken (EF) 38
Stewed Beef And Dumplings (PC) 96
Straw-Barb Juice (J) 83
Strawberry Daiquiri (B) 19
Strawberry Daiquiri, Virgin (B) 19
Strawberry Milk Shake (B) 15
Stroganoff, Turkey (EF) 43
Stuffed Apples, Spicy (PC) 110
Stuffed Mushrooms (TO) 139
Stuffing Meal, Chicken And (SC) 135
Sundried Tomato Pesto (B) 10
Sundried Tomato Pesto Spread (B) 10
Swedish Rye Bread (BM) 31
Sweet And Sour Chicken (PC) 97
Sweet And Sour Ribs (EF) 46
Sweet Potato Purée (FP) 65
Syrup, Very Berry (J) 88

Tartar Sauce (FP) 48
Tater Cakes, Lunchtime (SM) 116
Teriyaki Steak (SC) 133
Thin Pizza Crust (FP) 56
Toasts, S'more (SM) 120
Tomato Pesto Spread, Sundried (B) 10
Tomato Pesto, Sundried (B) 10
Treats
  Banana Toasties (SM) 120
  Berry Cheesy Sweet (SM) 121
  Mince Pie Singles (SM) 118
  Oriental Snack Mix (SC) 123
  Raisin Pies (SM) 119
  S'more Toasts (SM) 120
  Spicy Stuffed Apples (PC) 110
Tropical Breeze (J) 82
Tropical Loaf (J) 91
Tuna Sandwiches, Hot (SM) 114
Tuna Snack Buns (TO) 141
Turkey Patties (EF) 42
Turkey Stroganoff (EF) 43

Vegetable Beef Soup (PC) 94
Vegetable Brew, Orange (J) 81
Vegetable Pulp Soup (J) 86
Vegetable Topper (B) 11
Veggie Brew, Spicy (J) 85
Veggies Drink, Winter (J) 85
Very Berry Juice (J) 80
Very Berry Syrup (J) 88
Virgin Banana Daiquiri (B) 16
Virgin Strawberry Daiquiri (B) 19

Wheat Bread
  Cracked (BM) 28
  Honey (BM) .29
  Maple (BM) .25
Wheat Crust, Pizza (FP) 57
Wheat Pastry (FP) 61
White Cake (FP) 63
White Fruitcake (PC) 112
Whole Wheat Bread (BM) 28
Whole Wheat Twists (FP) 58
Wiener Snack Buns (TO) 141
Winter Veggies Drink (J) 85

Photo Index

A
Apricot Chicken 36

B
Baked Brie 143
Basil Pesto 71
Beef Bourguignon 126
Beefy Bun Topping. 125
Beet Bonanza. 89
Berry Cooler. 17
Berry Drink Concentrate. 72
Berry Rhubarb Dumpling
   Dessert . . . . Front Cover
Black Bean Soup. 71
Boston Brown Bread . . . . 35, Back Cover

C
Caesar Salad Dressing . . . . . . 35, Back Cover
Cheese Gnocchi. 53
Chicken Cacciatore. 107
Chicken Parmigiana 126
Chicken With Broccoli 144
Chili Snacks 108
Chinese Pepper Steak. 125
Chocolate Icing 54
Chocolate Pudding Cake 90
Cottage Dill Bread. . . . . 35, Back Cover
Crêpes 17
Crescent Pizza 144
Curried Beef And Barley. . . . . 35, Back Cover

D
Date Pie. 72

F
French Bread Pizza . . . . Front Cover
French-Type Dressing . . . . . . 35, Back Cover
Frozen Strawberry Daiquiri 17

G
Green Zinger 89

H
Herb Bread. 18
Hot Tuna Sandwiches. 108

L
Lasting Cereal Muffins 144
Lunchtime Tater Cakes 108

M
Maple Wheat Bread 18
Margarita Slush 17
Melon Drink. 72

Mixed Slaw 53
Monte Cristo Sandwich . . . . Front Cover

N
Navy Bean Soup. 107

O
Orange Poppy Seed Bread 18
Orange Vegetable Brew 89
Oriental Snack Mix. 143

P
Pizza Wheat Crust. 53
Poached Salmon 36
Pork Jambalaya. 107
Poutine. 144
Pumpernickel Bread 18

Q
Quick Salsa. 54

R
Rack Of Lamb. 90
Red Pepper Dip 71
Ribs Delight . . . . Front Cover

S
Seafood Canapés 143
S'more Toasts. 108
Shortbread. 54
Shrimp Cantonese 36
Shrimp Spread 71
Spaghetti Sauce And Meatballs. 126
Steak Bake 125
Stuffed Mushrooms 143
Sundried Tomato Pesto 18
Sundried Tomato Pesto Spread. 18

T
Tartar Sauce. 36
Teriyaki Steak 126
Tropical Breeze. . . . . Front Cover
Tropical Loaf. 72

V
Vegetable Beef Soup. 107
Very Berry Juice . . . . Front Cover
Very Berry Syrup. 17

W
White Cake. 54
White Fruitcake. 90
Whole Wheat Twists. 53
Winter Veggies Drink 89

156

Tip Index

A

Allowing space – in slow cooker 135
Avoiding spillage – with hand blender . . . 47

B

Basil, fresh – to freeze 68
Blender –
  controlling texture 10
  making bread crumbs 40
  making cracker crumbs 40
Bread crumbs – to make 40
Bread machine – make-ahead breads 40

C

Cheesecloth – using to strain juices 86
Coffee filter – using to strain juices 86
Controlling texture – in blender 10
Cracker crumbs – to make 40

F

Food Processor –
  getting even slices 50
  making bread crumbs 40
  making cracker crumbs 40
  slicing foods with peel 56
Foods not to be used – in pressure
  cooker 93
Freezing fresh basil 68

G

Getting clear juice 86
Getting even slices – in food processor . . . 50

H

Hand Blender –
  avoiding spillage 47
  mixing thoroughly 78

J

Juicer –
  getting clear juice 86
  saving vegetable pulp 59

M

Make–ahead breads 40
Making bread crumbs 40
Making cracker crumbs 40
Margarine – use in sandwich maker 111
Mixing thoroughly – in hand blender 78

P

Peel – slicing foods with 56
Pressure Cooker –
  foods not to be used in 93
  reducing cooking time in 103
  reducing pressure in 98
  using hard margarine in 111
Processing – large batches in blender 10
Protecting crock liner – of slow
  cooker 129

R

Reducing cooking time – in pressure
  cooker 103
Reducing pressure – in pressure
  cooker 98
Re-heating foil-wrapped food 147

S

Sandwich Maker – using margarine 111
Slicing food – in food processor 50, 56
Slow Cooker –
  allowing space 135
  protecting crock liner 129
Soup – using reserved vegetable pulp 59
Straining juices – using coffee filter 86
Straining juices – using cheesecloth 86

T

Toaster oven – re-heating foil-wrapped
  food 147

U

Using hard margarine – in pressure
  cooker 111

V

Vegetable pulp – using for soup 59

157

Company's Coming cookbooks are available at **retail locations** throughout Canada!

See mail order form

Buy any 2 cookbooks—choose a 3rd FREE of equal or less value than the lowest price paid.   *Available in Frenc

Original Series	CA$14.99 Canada		US$10.99 USA & International

CODE		CODE		CODE	
SQ	150 Delicious Squares*	DE	Desserts	PA	Pasta*
AP	Appetizers	KC	Kids Cooking*	PI	Pies*
AC	Appliance Cooking*	LCA	Light Casseroles*	PZ	Pizza!*
BA	Barbecues*	LR	Light Recipes*	PR	Preserves*
BR	Breads*	LFC	Low-Fat Cooking*	SA	Salads*
BB	Breakfasts & Brunches*	LFP	Low-Fat Pasta*	SC	Slow Cooker Recipes*
CK	Cakes	MC	Main Courses	SS	Soups & Sandwiches
CA	Casseroles*	MAM	Make-Ahead Meals*	ST	Starters*
CH	Chicken, Etc.*	ME	Meatless Cooking*	SF	Stir-Fry*
CO	Cookies*	MU	Muffins & More*	PB	The Potato Book*
CT	Cooking For Two*	ODM	One-Dish Meals*	VE	Vegetables

Greatest Hits	CA$12.99 Canada		US$9.99 USA & International

CODE		CODE		CODE	
BML	Biscuits, Muffins & Loaves*	ITAL	Italian* **NEW** *May 1/01*	SAW	Sandwiches & Wraps*
DSD	Dips, Spreads & Dressings*	MEX	Mexican* **NEW** *May 1/01*	SAS	Soups & Salads*

Lifestyle Series	CA$16.99 Canada		US$12.99 USA & International

CODE		CODE	
DC	Diabetic Cooking*	LFC	Low-fat Cooking*
GR	Grilling*	LFP	Low-fat Pasta*

Special Occasion Series	CA$19.99 Canada	US$19.99 USA & International

CODE	
CE	Chocolate Everything*

COOKBOOKS

www.**companys**coming.com
visit our web-site

COMPANY'S COMING PUBLISHING LIMITED
2311 - 96 Street
Edmonton, Alberta, Canada T6N 1G3
Tel: (780) 450-6223 Fax: (780) 450-1857

Exclusive Mail Order Offer

See page 158 for list of cookbooks

Buy 2 Get 1 FREE!
Buy any 2 cookbooks—choose a **3rd FREE**
of equal or less value than the lowest price paid.

Quantity	Code	Title	Price Each	Price Total
			$	$
		don't forget		
		to indicate your		
		free book(s).		
		(see exclusive mail order		
		offer above)		
		please print		

	TOTAL BOOKS (including FREE)	TOTAL BOOKS PURCHASED:	$

	International		Canada & USA	
Plus Shipping & Handling (per destination)	$7.00	(one book)	$5.00	(1-3 books)
Additional Books (including FREE books)	$	($2.00 each)	$	($1.00 each)
Sub-Total	$		$	
Canadian residents add G.S.T(7%)			$	
TOTAL AMOUNT ENCLOSED	$		$	

The Fine Print

- Orders outside Canada must be **PAID IN US FUNDS** by cheque or money order drawn on Canadian or US bank or by credit card.
- Make cheque or money order payable to: **COMPANY'S COMING PUBLISHING LIMITED**.
- Prices are expressed in Canadian dollars for Canada, US dollars for USA & International and are subject to change without prior notice.
- Orders are shipped surface mail. For courier rates, visit our web-site: **www.companyscoming.com** or contact us: **Tel: (780) 450-6223 Fax: (780) 450-1857**.
- Sorry, no C.O.D's.

☐ MasterCard   ☐ VISA

_____
Expiry date

Account # _____

Name of cardholder _____

Cardholder's signature _____

Gift Giving

- Let us help you with your gift giving!
- We will send cookbooks directly to the recipients of your choice if you give us their names and addresses.
- Please specify the titles you wish to send to each person.
- If you would like to include your personal note or card, we will be pleased to enclose it with your gift order.
- Company's Coming Cookbooks make excellent gifts: Birthdays, bridal showers, Mother's Day, Father's Day, graduation or any occasion...collect them all!

Shipping Address
Send the cookbooks listed above to:

Name: _____

Street: _____

City: _____ Prov./State: _____

Country: _____ Postal Code/Zip: _____

Tel: (_____)

E-mail address: _____

YES! Please send a catalogue: ☐ English ☐ French

Please mail or fax to:
Company's Coming Publishing Limited
2311 - 96 Street
Edmonton, Alberta, Canada   T6N 1G3
Fax: (780) 450-1857

Name:_____

Address:_____

_____

e-mail:_____

Reader Survey

We welcome your comments and would love to hear from you.
Please take a few moments to give us your feedback.

1. *Approximately what percentage of the cooking do you do in your home?*_____ %

2. *How many meals do you cook in your home in a typical week?*   _____

3. *How often do you refer to a cookbook (or other source) for recipes?*

❑ Everyday   ❑ 2 or 3 times a month   ❑ A few times a year
❑ A few times a week   ❑ Once a month   ❑ Never

4. *What recipe features are most important to you? Rank 1 to 7;*
   (1 being most important, 7 being least important).

_____ Recipes for everyday cooking
_____ Recipes for guests and entertaining
_____ Easy recipes; quick to prepare, with everyday ingredients
_____ Low-fat or health-conscious recipes
_____ Recipes you can trust to work
_____ Recipes using exotic ingredients
_____ Recipes using fresh ingredients only

5. *What cookbook features are most important to you? Rank 1 to 6;*
   (1 being most important, 6 being least important).

_____ Lots of color photographs of recipes
_____ "How-to" instructions or photos
_____ Helpful hints & cooking tips
_____ Lay-flat binding (coil or plastic comb)
_____ Well organized with complete index
_____ Priced low

6. *How many cookbooks have you purchased in the last year?*

7. *Of these, how many were gifts?*_____   _____

8. *Age group*

❑ Under 18   ❑ 25 to 34   ❑ 45 to 54   ❑ 65+
❑ 18 to 24   ❑ 35 to 44   ❑ 55 to 64

9. *What do you like best about Company's Coming Cookbooks?*

_____

_____

10. *How could Company's Coming Cookbooks be improved?*

_____

_____

11. *Topics you would like to see published by Company's Coming:*

_____

_____

Thank you for sharing your views. We truly value your input.